A NEW HISTORY OF SWANLAND

THE EIGHTEENTH AND NINETEENTH CENTURIES

Swanland Village History Group 2002

ISBN 0-9543440-0-6

Published by Swanland Village History Group

Printing Kindly Donated By :-

PPH Commercial
Chartered Surveyors
Commercial Property Consultants
The Hesslewood Estate
Ferriby Road, Hessle, HU13 0LG
Tel 01482 648888
www.pph-commercial.co.uk

We are also grateful for a kind donation from :-
The Sir James Reckitt Charity

And a loan from :-
Swanland Village Association

Binding by Colin Burnham 01482 509860

ACKNOWLEDGEMENTS

Our thanks are due to the many individuals whose works are listed in this document. In particular we would like to express our gratitude to David and Susan Neave for their assistance in the dating of Mere House and Swanland's 17th century cottages, to Janice and Peter Crowther for their permission to quote extensively from the Diary of Robert Sharp, and to Dr Basil Reckitt for quotations from the history of his family's business.

We are most grateful to numerous others who have helped us by providing photographs and documents and encouraging us in our endeavours.

Thanks are also due to the following organisations for the opportunity to access materials in their care:

Beverley Reference Library
The Borthwick Institute, York
The British Library, London
Christ Church, Swanland
The East Riding Local History Society
The East Riding Registry of Deeds
The East Riding of Yorkshire Archives
Hull City Archives
Hull College
Hull Local Studies Library
Holy Trinity Church, Hull
Humberside Archaeological Partnership
The Public Record Office, London
The Reckitt Benkiser Archives
The University of Hull Archives

In particular we would like to thank the East Riding of Yorkshire Archives and the Hull Local Studies Library for permission to reproduce certain of their maps, the Hull Local Studies Library for permission to use extracts from the *Autobiography of Thomas Blossom* and *Executors Accounts for Samuel Galland*, and the University of Hull for including extracts from the *Papers of the Andrew Family*. We are indebted to Hull City Archives for access to Land and Window Tax Returns and to Christ Church, Swanland for access to J E Whitehead's *Records of the Congregational Church*.

PREFACE

The idea of compiling a new history of Swanland originated in the millennium year. The assembly of a thousand years of village history seemed appropriate to this anniversary, but in the event, the short timescale precluded publication. A number of interested villagers got together and began to assemble information and articles to create an archive, which would form the basis of a subsequent history.

Researching the documents took those involved to the local studies libraries at Beverley and Hull, and to archive offices in Beverley, Leeds, and the City and University of Hull. Visits were made to the British Library and the Public Record Office in London. Kind offerings of photographs and other documents were received from villagers and assistance obtained from lecturers in local history at the University of Hull. The resulting history that begins below is extensively referenced to these sources as an aid to those working in the field in future years.

It was decided to publish the history in parts. This had a number of advantages. Each member of the History Group was able to focus on a particular period or topic, the time to publishing the initial part was foreshortened and individual parts were made more affordable. The following document is the first part to be issued and covers the eighteenth and nineteenth centuries. It is hoped that later parts will refer to the medieval period, Tudor and Stuart times, the twentieth century, and the growth of the church and education in Swanland.

Although topics were researched and discussed by all the members of the group, each chapter has mainly been the responsibility of one or two.

The compilers of the present part were Linda Collier, (The Eighteenth Century), and John Holmes & Shirley Dalby, (The Nineteenth Century). The other members of the group were Derek Brooks, Yvonne Dumsday, and Glenys Thompson

It would be remiss to conclude this preface without mention of the excellent *Recollections of Village Life* published some years ago by J & C A Wheeler. It is hoped that the present publication will be seen as complementary to their work.

CONTENTS

LIST OF ILLUSTRATIONS

Page

APPENDICES

1. Window Tax Records for Swanland, 1774 and 1779

2. Land Tax Records for Swanland, 1791 and 1797

3. A Swanland Rental for 1779

4. Village Occupations

5. Deaths in Swanland, 1808 - 1851

THE EIGHTEENTH CENTURY

INTRODUCTION

From a national viewpoint, the eighteenth century is notable as a time of accelerating change, a process that has continued unabated from then on. The latter part of the century, in particular, is often referred to by historians as 'the age of enlightenment', which saw radical developments in European thought and culture with particular emphasis on the human capacity for logical thought and the advancement of knowledge. This, in turn, gradually led to more efficient working practices in all areas of endeavour and to slowly improving social conditions.

Despite Britain's involvement in costly wars, international trade developed rapidly, and with it port cities such as Hull. The merchants of its High Street prospered mightily and its population, of around 7,500 in the year 1700, almost quadrupled during the ensuing century with the arrival of more and more newcomers.[1]

In the village of Swanland, however, the effects of these developments were felt much more gradually and the major change in agricultural practice, which was happening elsewhere as a result of the enclosure movement, was not achieved here until well into the following century. Nevertheless, the building of Swanland Hall by a wealthy Hull merchant marked the first arrival in the village by a successful man of commerce who had identified it as a highly desirable location for his country residence.

This account of eighteenth century Swanland has been written from the perspective of the Georgian period as a whole. The stories of Swanland Hall and Thomas Blossom are continued beyond the end of the century, and the sections on the open fields and the roads anticipate the changes that were to occur at the time of enclosure.

POPULATION

Swanland in the eighteenth century was still a small, but gradually expanding, rural community. The Window Tax return of 1774[2] mentions 49 households, compared to only 35 in the Hearth Tax return of 1672.[3] Of these 35, only 13 of the families (some inter-related) are still identifiable by name as being still resident in the village a century later. However, the surnames of Galland, Shaw, Todd, Turner and Watson occur repeatedly in the surviving records of the period, and the original deeds[4] of 1694 for the chapel and school name two Watsons and a Turner amongst the trustees.

The basis of the local economy remained entirely agricultural and, though the open field system still prevailed, rudimentary agricultural machinery began to be employed locally. Windmills were built, and Thomas Blossom,[5] writing of Thomas Chapman (with whom he completed his apprenticeship in 1798 after the death of his first master) mentions him as "the first man to make a threshing machine in this part of the Country".

JOHN PORTER AND SWANLAND HALL

John Porter was an important merchant trading with Russia[6] and, at first, lived close to his business in High Street in Hull.

It was in 1740, according to Allison,[7] that the Porters bought land in Swanland and in due course built Swanland Hall. If the land was indeed bought in that year it can hardly have been John himself who was the purchaser, since he was then only nine years of age. It is not known from whom the land was purchased or who constructed the Hall. The mansion is listed in the Window Tax returns of 1774 and 1779[2] as having forty-one windows, by far the greatest number of any building in the village.

Fig. 1   Swanland Hall in 2001:
the central block as built for John Porter,
the outer wings being added at a later date.

John Porter appears[8] to have been born in Hull in 1731, son of Francis Porter, master mariner and merchant,[9] and his wife Elizabeth Blaydes.   It may be that this connection with the wealthy merchant family of Blaydes was the beginning of the Porters' rising fortune.   John married Jane Thornton, the daughter of another Hull merchant, on 17 July 1756 in Holy Trinity Church, Hull.[8]   Merchant families had close business relationships, often cemented by marriage between members of the families.   The Wilberforce, Thornton, Etherington and Pease families were closely related in this way.

John was the Sheriff of Hull in 1759 and Mayor in 1770 and in 1778.   Documents in the Hull City Record Office refer to Alderman Porter's agreement[10] with a firm to build a new bridge over the River Hull in April 1785, to repairs of staithes at his own expense[11] and to the lease of Salter's Lane Staithes and Sufferance Quay (for five shillings per year payable in October) for 21 years from September 1785.   His mayoral expenses,[12] paid 4 January 1771 and 8 July 1771, were £32 10s on each account.

As Mayor in 1771, he accepted the resignation[13] of William Wilberforce the elder (grandfather of the MP of that name) after 48 years in office as Alderman. In 1775, John Porter was a signatory, as an Alderman, to a loyal address[14] sent by the Mayor, Recorder and Aldermen of Hull to George III, concerning the war in America, and delivered by Henry Etherington,[15] who was created baronet the same year.

In 1774 Porter was an original subscriber, having one share of £250, in the making of a dock at the port of Hull[16] later to be known as Queen's Dock. The dock was an immediate success with the first dividend in 1781 issued at £52 per share.

John and his wife, Jane, had two children: a son, also John, born in 1758, and a daughter, Jane, born in 1761, both of whom were baptised in Holy Trinity Church, Hull.[17]

An indication of his property holdings in Swanland is given by the Land Tax return of 1791,[18] which lists him as liable for the fifth highest rate in the township. In addition to Swanland Hall and its grounds, he held Bullock Farm, Nicholson Close, Bradley Close, Fowler Close, part of Pease Farm and part of Norrison Farm.

In his will of 21 January 1793,[19] the year of his death, he requested that he be buried in the vault in Holy Trinity Church, Hull, next to his father. This vault actually lies in the churchyard, between the south door of the church and the choir vestry. His son John died in the December of the same year, aged 35 years, and also lies in the family vault. On the death of his wife, Jane, in 1812, his daughter, also Jane, wife of James Walker of Beverley, inherited his estate. Jane and James Walker had two daughters, Jane and Harriet, and one son, James. Harriet married Joseph Robinson Pease, son of a Hull Merchant, and Jane married a Mr. Hill. James, the son, was married twice, firstly to Mary Denison and secondly to Marie Thompson. He was created a baronet in 1868[20] and his third son (the great grandson of John Porter) was Admiral Charles Francis Walker, after whom Admiral Walker Road in Beverley is named. There are memorial plaques and commemorative windows to the Walker family in Beverley Minister.

While in Hull, John Porter lived on the west side of High Street,[21] with land and property in Myton extending over what became Porter Street, Walker Street, Hill Street and Pease Street: all streets laid out in memory of family members.

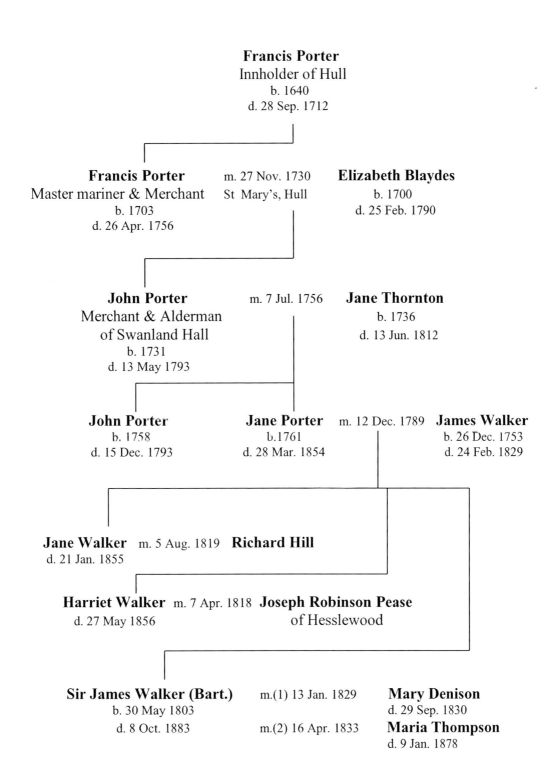

Francis Porter
Innholder of Hull
b. 1640
d. 28 Sep. 1712

Francis Porter   m. 27 Nov. 1730   **Elizabeth Blaydes**
Master mariner & Merchant   St Mary's, Hull   b. 1700
b. 1703   d. 25 Feb. 1790
d. 26 Apr. 1756

John Porter   m. 7 Jul. 1756   **Jane Thornton**
Merchant & Alderman   b. 1736
of Swanland Hall   d. 13 Jun. 1812
b. 1731
d. 13 May 1793

John Porter   **Jane Porter**   m. 12 Dec. 1789   **James Walker**
b. 1758   b.1761   b. 26 Dec. 1753
d. 15 Dec. 1793   d. 28 Mar. 1854   d. 24 Feb. 1829

Jane Walker   m. 5 Aug. 1819   **Richard Hill**
d. 21 Jan. 1855

Harriet Walker   m. 7 Apr. 1818   **Joseph Robinson Pease**
d. 27 May 1856   of Hesslewood

Sir James Walker (Bart.)   m.(1) 13 Jan. 1829   **Mary Denison**
b. 30 May 1803   d. 29 Sep. 1830
d. 8 Oct. 1883   m.(2) 16 Apr. 1833   **Maria Thompson**
                                                                 d. 9 Jan. 1878

Fig. 2 A Porter Family Tree

Here lieth the body of
Francis Porter
of this town, Innholder,
who departed this life
the 28th day of September 1712
in the 72nd year of his age.

Also
Francis Porter,
Merchant
who *obit* 26 April 1756
aged 53 years
and **Elizabeth,** his wife,
who departed this life
25 February 1790
aged 90 years.

John Porter Esq.
Obit 13 May 1793, aged 62,
who served twice in the office of
Mayor of this Corporation

Also **John Porter Esq.**
son of the above John Porter Esq.,
who departed this life
15 December 1793, aged 35 years.

Fig. 3 A transcript of the inscriptions on the Porter family vault in Holy Trinity churchyard, Hull

(Author's note: The surfaces of the stones have been much abraded recently by the storage and movement of building materials within the churchyard in connection with the restoration of the church tower. The inscriptions are now, in parts, almost illegible.)

As already indicated, John Porter's estate passed, on the death of his widow in 1812, to his daughter, Jane Walker and her husband James. They in turn, in 1818, sold the Hall to Nicholas Sykes.[22] The deeds describe a Mansion House with coach houses, stables, offices and other outbuildings, gardens, orchard, hot houses, plantations, fish ponds, trees, woods and underwoods comprising 14 acres 3 roods and 15 perches. In the deeds the estate is said to be "late in tenure or occupation of Mr Thomas Hall or his undertenants", so presumably Thomas Hall rented the property for some time between Mrs Porter's death and the sale in 1818.

The Sykes family lived in the Hall from 1818 until the Sykes Trustees sold it, after the death of Nicholas Sykes, to John Todd[23, 24] of Swanland on the 9 October 1830. The Trustees were: Nicholas' wife Mary, daughters Julia Lucy, Mary Anne and Ann, sons Daniel the elder of Raywell, Richard the younger of Westella, Joseph of Kirkella, Frederick of Cottingham and married daughters and their husbands, Mr Matthew and Mrs Frances Babington, Mr Joseph and Mrs Sophie Wilkinson, the Rev Henry and Mrs Martha Venn of Drypool (whose academic son John (1834-1923) invented the Venn diagrams[25]). In due course Mary Sykes and her daughters Julia Lucy, Mary Anne and Ann went to live in Cheltenham.

The Todd family, already landowners in Swanland, remained owners of the Hall until 1926. The bill of sale of the Swanland Hall Estate, including the Hall with its 44.117 acres, gives the total area of the estate as 708 acres, to be sold in a number of separate lots. The village benefited greatly from the Todds' patronage and an account of the family is given in the chapter covering the 19th century.

The Barton family followed the Todds as occupants of the Hall and demolished the north wing. In 1947 Mr and Mrs Clayton became the owners of the Hall and, after Mr. Clayton's death, his widow sold some of the surrounding land to pay for death duties. From her husband's death until her own death in 1979 Mrs Clayton lived alone, employing only a few staff to maintain the place. She left a will containing instructions for the demolition of the Hall after her demise, but this was circumvented by the building being listed as one of special historic and architectural interest and, in 1983, the Environment Secretary of the day, Patrick Jenkins, confirmed refusal for its demolition.

Ivan Hall of Beverley, a local historian, described[26] the Hall as "a transplant of the big merchants' houses of Hull, having the same sort of craft work in its fireplaces and on the staircases". In 1980 it is specified[26] as "a three storey building with eight bedrooms and three bathrooms, in need of re-roofing and re-plumbing at a cost estimated (in1975) at £70,000". A sorry state of decay for what had once been the grandest house in the village.

Generations of Swanland children and adults had regulated their lives by the striking of the clock on the stable block of the Hall.

Fig. 4 The Stable Clock, Swanland Hall

In August 1980, Beverley Planning Committee approved plans by Knyman and Hurd to build eight bungalows and ten houses on five acres of the adjoining land, now Hall Park. In 1984, the Hall itself was acquired by Martin White, who ultimately obtained planning permission for its conversion into eight luxury apartments.

OTHER HOUSES AND LANDHOLDINGS
IN EIGHTEENTH CENTURY SWANLAND

Houses

There is no definitive map or list showing all the houses that existed in the village in the eighteenth century, but records do survive which give at least some indication of the extent of the built environment at that time.

Wheeler and Wheeler[27] have discussed a number of buildings that dated from Georgian times or earlier. These include:

the Priory Farmhouse, once thought to have been built during the Elizabethan period though it is more likely to date from William and Mary, on a site near the entrance to the present Mere Way, and demolished after the Second World War;

the Old Parsonage, which still stands in West End;

according to one author,[28] the first Manor House, built in 1695 by John Parker Lord of the Manor, and demolished in the nineteenth century;

the Dower House, possibly also dating from the seventeenth century, and demolished in 1963, which stood at the entrance to what is now Dower Rise; and

Toft House, on Main Street.

According to Patton,[29] the Old Parsonage was built in 1696 on land granted and conveyed by John Turner on a site abutting his grounds on the south and those of Sir Griffith Boynton (Bart.) on the west. The house has been altered many times and in 1855 John Todd had its east end heightened. The original deeds for chapel and school of 1694 name one of the trustees as William Watson. Several family names such as Watson, Turner, Galland, Shaw and Todd keep appearing on the various documents.

Patton[30] refers to the Dower House having an ancient barn some 700 years old, and Wheeler and Wheeler[31] describe the house as having rooms on three floors and large cellars, also gable ends showing a design of brickwork known as tumble gabling. Further examples of tumble gabling can be seen on the house at the junction of West End and Kemp Road and on the cottage block opposite.

Fig. 5 Eighteenth Century Tumble Gabling
In this example the triangular arrays of inclined bricks can be seen at
two levels, the height of the building having been raised at some time

Other houses known to have existed in the eighteenth century include the present Post Office in West End, which has the date of 1721 over the door and was allegedly built by Isaac Lupton, together with the adjoining Boulder Cottage.

Fig. 6 Date stone above the lintel
of the present Swanland Post Office

Of the more modest dwellings, Holgate Cottages (numbers 20 to 28 Main Street) probably also date from the eighteenth century, having been modernised in the 1980s while retaining their original shell. The pantiled whitewashed shops opposite the northern end of Kemp Road were cottages that certainly existed in the eighteenth century and even earlier.

Other farm workers' houses of that period along Main Street and Dale Road have all been demolished in the course of the last two hundred years.

The Land Tax and Window Tax Records

'But in this world
nothing can be said to be certain
except death and taxes'.
Benjamin Franklin, 1789

'All taxes must, at last,
fall upon agriculture'.
Edward Gibbon 1788

The Land Tax returns[18, 32] of 1791 and 1797 give some indication of the persons holding land in the area at that time (see Appendix 2), though Ginter[33] has outlined the problems encountered in the interpretation of these data. For example, it is not always clear whether the farms are owned or tenanted.

In 1791,[18] the most highly rated holding in Swanland (at a rateable value of £45) was that of John Ringrose, 'for his farm and tithe', though Ringrose also held Pickering Farm, together with Sir Henry Etherington's part of Pease Farm, for which he paid additional taxes. (The rate payable was four shillings per pound of rateable value).

Thomas Shaw, for Lillingston Farm, was rated at £43.13.6, and for his own farm £12.13.4, also £5.13.4 for part of Briershill Farm, and £1 for tithe of Humber Close. Robert Todd's tithe was £33.16.8, and £43.13.6 for Julie's Wood Farm and Dama [*sic*] Farm, with £1 for Cockcroft and meadow. John Porter was taxed for his Hall and grounds along with part of Pease Farm, part of Norrison's Farm, Bullock Farm, Nicholson Close, Bradley Close and Fowler Close. By the time of the enclosure, Porter's Hall and lands were in the hands of John Todd.

It will be noted that, in some cases, different people held separate pieces of the same farm: for example Henry Watson and John Turner each had parts of Pease Farm and John Porter and John Turner parts of Norrison Farm.

At the lower end of the scale John Blossom, whose son Thomas became a missionary (*q.v.*), is taxed in 1791 for his house at 10 shillings, as was S Atkinson, and Thomas Brigham for his house at 15 shillings. Several small pieces of land were taxed at £1.5.0.

A better snapshot of the various dwellings in the village is given by the Window Tax returns[2] (see Appendix 1). This tax, as the name suggests, was based on the number of windows in a building and is an indication of the size of the property.

In the Window Tax for Swanland of 1774, Swanland Hall had 41 windows, with the next properties in size having 15 and 11. Four was the lowest number of windows on which tax was paid, and the poor were exempt. In the 1774 return, 49 names are listed and, in 1779, 43 names. Between 1774 and 1779 there were few changes. George Hall had added another window. John Bullock is listed instead of William Bullock. John Featherstone had four windows and Thomas Featherstone had become poor. Often windows were blocked off to avoid paying tax. Evidence of this was at one time discernible in Swanland on Toft House and the present Post Office, both of which had upstairs windows bricked up.

THOMAS BLOSSOM

Growing up in Swanland

The history of the Independent Chapel in Swanland is dealt with elsewhere, but no account of Swanland during the Georgian period would be complete without reference to one of its most devoted youthful members. Thomas Blossom, the first of eight children of John and Ann Blossom, was born in Swanland in or about July 1777. He claimed to have been baptised by the Rev Samuel Bottomley who was Minister of the Independent Chapel at a time when it suffered a serious split in its congregation in the early 1770s. As the date of the baptism is recorded as 18 July 1777, it is possible that this was an occasion of a return visit by Bottomley to his former flock, since by that time he had already moved on to a new ministry in Scarborough.[34]

About 1847, at around 70 years of age, Blossom wrote an account of some of the "many kind dispensations of Providence ..... bestowed on me, ... that my dear boy"[his son, Joseph] "may have the pleasure of reviewing the goodness of God towards myself ..." This is a very detailed personal account of a remarkable and eventful life. A copy, transcribed by hand some fifty years later from the original manuscript, then in the possession of Blossom's son, is deposited in the Hull Local Studies Library.[35] The early part of the story gives some interesting insights into life in Swanland in the late eighteenth century.

Family tradition had it that one of Thomas's ancestors was an active soldier in the parliamentary army in the reign of Charles I and may well have fought under Oliver Cromwell at the battle of Marston Moor.[36]

Be that as it may, his paternal grandfather, also Thomas Blosssom, married Ellen Lammin, a blacksmith's daughter from Winteringham in Lincolnshire and had ten children. He was a considerable farmer at Brantingham Thorpe House in East Yorkshire but, owing to disease among the cattle and sheep, he suffered much reduced circumstances from which he failed to recover.[37]

Thomas's mother, Ann Stephenson, was born in Barton-upon-Humber, daughter of Richard Stephenson (carpenter and joiner) and his wife, both of whom died when their family was young, leaving the eldest son, William, to take over the business and the welfare of the other five family members.[38] Thomas Blossom had a great affection for his mother's family, and it was his mother who saw to it that her children regularly accompanied her to the Chapel, his father being "a man that paid but little attention to these things".[39]

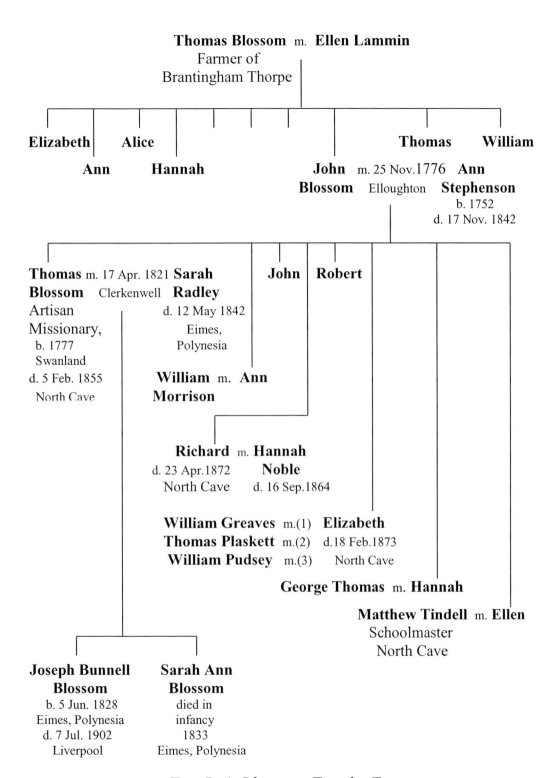

Fig. 7 A Blossom Family Tree

Thomas was sent "very early" to the village school where he learnt spelling, reading the scriptures, writing and arithmetic under Mr Peter Hodsman, to whom he became very attached. The education was geared to fit the sons and daughters of the farming and labouring classes for their role in life. Thomas could only attend during winter months, being employed in helping his father in his business during the summer. His uncle, Mr. William Birks, was the teacher at Ferriby and, since the Lillingston family of Ferriby had endowed education for six boys from Swanland, Thomas attended at Ferriby for two years; but he did not like it or progress as well as at Swanland. He left Ferriby and had one more winter of school at Swanland, leaving at about the age of twelve.[40]

Meanwhile he had been helping his father, whose business was that of a jobber (wholesale dealer) in cattle and other livestock. "And so", as he himself put it, "I entered into the *honourable* calling of a cattle drover, which I most abominably hated, and many a time swore vengence [*sic*] against it".[41] Nevertheless, the work required his attendance at fairs and markets and mingling with strangers, and this experience encouraged him to shed his natural shyness. No doubt it also imbued him with a sense of shrewdness and fair dealing.

About this time, when Thomas was some thirteen years old, he was also charged with looking after his father's two horses, which were loaned out to friends and neighbours from time to time. It was in this connection that he first encountered Thomas Marshall, an old friend of his father who had recently returned from the Americas to take over the village business of wheelwright and joiner – the business in which, some years earlier, he had served his apprenticeship. It is clear that Marshall took a liking to young Blossom and asked him whether he could recommend any likely lad who might wish to join him as an apprentice. "I said I could – and directly recommended myself! He replied that he would be very glad of it if my father was agreeable to it. I told him that there was no fear of that, and that I should be at his shop at six o'clock on Monday morning".

This assertion, however, stemmed more from bravado than well founded confidence, and John Blossom's initial reaction was one of anger when his eldest son informed him that Friday night that he was going to a new situation on the following Monday. Nevertheless, when the nature of the job was explained to him, he agreed that Thomas might go to Marshall on a month's trial. Thomas writes: "I staid a month and, as I liked it very much, I was bound apprentice for seven years to an agricultural wheelwright and joiner. The terms were that I was to have board, washing, lodging and a pair of new shoes every year".[42]

Following representations by his uncle, William Birks of Ferriby, and by Rev Joseph Milner of Hull, Thomas succeeded in qualifying for "Cogan's County", an award for apprentices to the mechanical and sea trades provided for in Alderman Cogan's will.[43] Apprentices were bound free of expenses and were to have £1 a year during their apprenticeship. On completion, a certificate from the master entitled the apprentice to a payment of £4 and the master, £2.

Sadly, before the completion of Thomas Blossom's apprenticeship, his master, Thomas Marshall died of consumption. His widow (for by then he had married a local girl and had two children) sold the business to a Mr Chapman, a skilful craftsman who, according to Blossom, was the first man in the district to make a threshing machine. Under the terms of the sale Mrs Marshall was to receive payment of 7 shillings per week for the two years Thomas had left to serve, *i.e.* some £36 in total, a tidy sum in those days. In the event, she died soon after her husband and, in the interim, their children had also died of the whooping cough. "So", writes Thomas poignantly, "that in the course of six months I made coffins for the Master, the Mistress and two children".

Mrs Marshall's executor was her father, Thomas Shaw, a wealthy farmer who was no friend to the Blossom family. The young Blossom was most aggrieved by the realisation that he would now be toiling to generate additional income for Mr Shaw, and it was only after some serious disagreements, eventually resolved by the Cogan trustees, that he continued to serve out his time with Mr Chapman.

The trustees ruled that, while Shaw was quite entitled to the seven shillings per week, he would not receive the final £2, normally paid to the master on completion of the apprenticeship, since neither master had acted for the full seven-year term. This decision had incensed Shaw, who then privately indicated to Blossom that he would expect him to hand over the £4 payable to the apprentice.

On the final day of his apprenticeship, Blossom requested and received a certificate of fulfilment of the terms from Mr Chapman. He then tricked Shaw's son-in-law into giving him the copy of his indentures, so immediately enabling him to claim the £4 bounty which he flatly refused to hand over to the furious Shaw. "On my return", Blossom writes , "when my friends found that I had so completely got over the old man (for he was no favourite), they would have set the bells ringing, but we happened to have none in Swanland".

Throughout this time Thomas was a regular attender at the Chapel, where the Rev David Williams made a lasting impression on the young man. Under his direction Thomas was instrumental in setting up the Sunday School of the Independents in Swanland, on the lines of the model established by Robert Raikes in Gloucester in

1789, and became its leading young teacher. Wherever in England his subsequent travels were to take him, Thomas always joined a Chapel and, in many places, started Sunday Schools.[44]

Some six months after completing his apprenticeship Thomas, now a journeyman joiner, decided it was time to broaden his horizons and, in the tradition of journeymen, to move on to pastures new.[45] He discussed his plans with his close friend from the Chapel, Thomas Ward, a serious and thoughtful lad who still had six months to serve in his apprenticeship to a blacksmith. He also went to talk to his parents who, since 1795, were living at North Cave. At first his mother tried to dissuade him from leaving the district and urged him to go and work with Mr Holborn, the joiner at North Cave, but to no avail. Thomas promised, however, that he would let them know his whereabouts as soon as he found work.

At about 11.00pm on the night of Sunday 12 August 1798, Thomas Ward crept out of his master's house, forsaking his apprenticeship, and set out with his friend Blossom to seek employment elsewhere. They walked all night and by eight o'clock the following morning they were within four miles of York, where they quickly found work. Separately, they also found comfortable lodgings with good Methodist families.

Abroad in the wider world

At this time, however, one of the hazards to which a young man might be subjected, to the disruption of his career plans, was a requirement to serve in the militia. This military reserve had been re-established by Act of Parliament some forty years previously[46] and was largely manned by a form of conscription. Parishes were required to maintain lists of adult males from which names were drawn by ballot to furnish the required number of men. In 1798, at the beginning of the Napoleonic Wars, militiamen faced an uncertain future.

After Blossom and his companion had been working in York for a few weeks, he chanced to overhear a conversation which implied that his name had been drawn in the ballot at York. Without waiting for the warrant to be served, he and Thomas Ward took the coach for Tadcaster and thence to Doncaster, "giving them the privilege of drawing another man in my place".

Finding no employment in Doncaster, the pair walked (the same day) to Bawtry and thence to nearby Misson, where they were hired to work on the Bawtry to Stockwith canal - rough work but, in the circumstances, welcome.[47] In due course Thomas moved on successively to Sheffield, Derby, Nottingham, Lichfield, Birmingham and London.[48]

Fig. 8 Thomas Blossom (from a drawing of 1821)

In London he worked in the more exacting trade of coachbuilding (at which he had first had an opportunity to try his hand while in Sheffield) and had two unsuccessful attempts at starting his own business.[49] All this time he remained a devout Christian and eventually, while attending a prayer meeting, he learned that the London Missionary Society was sending people out to the South Seas and wanted a worker "in the wood line". He volunteered and was accepted.[50] He was advised to go out as a married man and therefore proposed to Sarah Radley, whom he married on 17 April 1821 at Clerkenwell Church.[51] Before leaving the country he made farewell visits to members of his family and friends, some of whom he never saw again.

On 5. May 1821 Thomas and Sarah sailed on the South Seas whaler *Tuscan* in the company of the Rev Daniel Tyreman, Mr George Bennett, Mr and Mrs Jones and Mr and Mrs Armitage. The voyage of 20,000 miles to Tahiti took 4½ months.[52] During his many years on the islands, Thomas worked as an artisan missionary, moving around to wherever his skills were needed, building houses and chapels, making furniture, repairing ships and teaching various trades to the islanders. In 1828 Sarah and Thomas had a son, Joseph[53] and in 1833 a daughter, who lived only a very short time and was buried on the island of Eimes,[54] to be joined in 1842 by her mother.[55]

Some time later there was a period of unrest, with hostilities between the Queen and the people of Taiarabu. Twenty people were killed, and the natives of Eromanga murdered two Englishmen. The French, who were keen to have the Islands under French rule, took the initiative and landed 500 troops, driving the Queen from her home and taking the British Consul prisoner. The British government did not offer sufficient support at this time.[56]

Thomas Blossom decided that it was time to return home with Joseph. They left on 10 January 1844 on the American ship *William and Eliza*,[57] travelling via Rio de Janiero to New York, and from New York to Liverpool on the ship *Sheffield*. Thomas had a sister living in Liverpool, where his Tahitian dress caused some amusement and embarrassment. After 23 years away, Thomas returned to East Yorkshire, delighted to renew contact with friends and relatives but saddened to find that "many had fallen asleep".[58]

Joseph went off to the Mission School in Walthamstow for two years, spending the last six months as an assistant teacher, and ultimately secured a job in York in the Lancashire and Yorkshire Railway office.[59]

Thomas Blossom spent the first twenty years of his life in Swanland, gaining a simple education and learning a craft, but in the forty-six years he was away from the area he travelled great distances, lived a life rich in experience and served his God in many diverse ways. He died on 5th February 1855 and is buried in the churchyard at North Cave.

*Fig. 9 Thomas Blossom's Grave at North Cave
(for a transcript of the inscription, see overleaf)*

The inscription reads:

IN AFFECTIONATE REMEMBRANCE OF
THOMAS BLOSSOM.
AS AN EMBASSADOR FOR CHRIST
HE LABOURED AMONGST THE
HEATHEN OF TAHITI AND EIMES IN
POLYNESIA FOR 23 YEARS
IN CONNECTION WITH THE
LONDON MISSIONARY SOCIETY
AND, AFTER A LIFE
CHARACTERISED BY CHRISTIAN
CONSISTENCY, HAVING SERVED HIS
OWN GENERATION, BY THE WILL OF
GOD HE FELL ASLEEP
IN THIS PARISH
ON 5TH FEBRY. 1855, AGED 77 YEARS.

ALSO IN MEMORY OF
JOSEPH BUNNELL BLOSSOM
SON OF THE ABOVE
BORN IN TAHITI 5TH JUNE 1828
DIED IN LIVERPOOL 4TH JULY 1902
AGED 74 YEARS

THE OPEN FIELDS

Beatus ille, qui ……　　　　　　　　　　*Happy the man who……*
paterna rura　　　　　　　　　　　　　　*tills his ancestral fields*
bubus exercet suis　　　　　　　　　　　　*with his own oxen*
　　　　　　　　　　　　　　　　　　　Horace (65 to 8BC)

In Georgian times the basis of the local economy, in common with that of the rest of the East Riding, was agriculture. Parliamentary Enclosure was not completed in Swanland until 1837, so it was not until the decade following the end of the Georgian period that the full effects of the enclosure movement were experienced.

Many of the dwellings built along the main street would have been single story buildings, and the occupants, without exception, were engaged in agriculture or its supporting services. Before enclosure, the Open Field System still prevailed, whereby each township or village operated a three- or four-field system according to the type of soil, allowing a crop and fallow rotation to be worked communally. Swanland had a four-field system, with *North Field* to the north-east of Main Street and Dale Road, *South Field* to the south-east of Main Street and Kemp Road, *Humber Field* still further to the south-east and extending to the river, and *West Field* (from which West Field Farm and West Field Lane take their names) to the north-west of Mill Road and Dale Road.

A fifth field, *Wold Field*, to the south-west of Mill Road and West Leys Road, belonged to the township of Ferriby. All these old names were still apparent on the Ordnance Survey map of 1855.

Each arable field was divided into long rectangular sections, or 'furlongs' (also known locally as 'flats'[60]), by 'balks', or grassy strips, which not only marked the boundaries but also served as paths and for grazing.[61] The furlong of 220 yards, as a measure of length, was so called because it was about the average length of a ploughed furrow in the open field; and the balks were often given individual names, as can be seen from the pre-enclosure map of Swanland of 1824.[62] Town End Balk, Rose Balk, West Porter Balk and a variety of other highly evocative names all add local interest.

The furlongs were further divided lengthways into narrow strips, (also known as 'lands') each individually held, with each landholder having a number of strips scattered amongst the various open fields to allow for the crop rotation system. Repeated ploughing over a long period of time resulted in the long edges of the strips standing out in relief above the ploughed areas ('ridge and furrow')[63] and in a corresponding build up of earth at the end of each furrow ('the headland').[64]

In some places these long established ridge and furrow patterns are still to be seen, usually in meadow land where they have not fallen victim to deep ploughing.

Of course, the cultivation of a number of often widely scattered strips was very inefficient in terms of time and effort, and it was the wish for consolidation of their holdings on the part of the major landholders within a township that was often the driving force behind Parliamentary Enclosure.

A further refinement of the Open Field System was the infield/outfield arrangement.[65] Livestock would usually be kept on land close to the dwellings, and it was on this land that the manure would be spread. This land, known as the infield, would thereby become more fertile and suitable for the growing of grain such as wheat or barley. The land further away from the homesteads, the outfield, being less fertile, was allowed to lie fallow for longer and, while fallow, would be used for common grazing. In the latter part of the eighteenth century the crop/fallow practices in numerous East Riding communities were subject to some change as a result of the introduction of turnip growing, largely to provide additional animal feed.[66]

During the period 1745 to 1750 there was an outbreak of cattle plague and attempts were made to restrict the normal movement of stock.[67] Thomas Blossom refers to his grandfather being much reduced in circumstances "owing to a great murrain amongst the cattle".[37]

THE VILLAGE MILL

For a farming community the mill was a very important facility. The earliest type of windmill was the post mill, in which the body and machinery were balanced on a central post and the sails were turned into the wind by manhandling a pole at the rear. The only surviving local example is at Wrawby in North Lincolnshire.

North Ferriby had such a mill which also served Swanland before the village had its own facility:

> "The Ferriby Mill, newly erected, together with half an acre of land, was sold by Robert Harness of Melton to Watson Stickney, a miller of Welton, in February 1761. The mill was then occupied by Thomas Todd, although by 1779 Richard Stephenson seems to have been the occupant".[68]

It is shown on Thomas Jefferys' map of 1775,[69] on a site north of the junction of Kemp Road with West Leys Road which, at that time, lay just outside the Swanland boundary. The mill is listed in the North Ferriby Land Tax return of 1773 and is assessed at £3.10.0, with a rate of three shillings in the pound resulting in a levy of 10s 6d.

Fig. 10 Ferriby Mill (from a contemporary painting)

Ferriby Mill remained in use until 1876, when it was demolished on the instructions of Robert Brough Watson.

On Greenwood's map of 1817[70] two mills are shown: the Ferriby Mill and the Swanland Mill. The latter is located at the western end of the village, on the northern side of Mill Hill near its junction with Woodgates Lane and Mill Road

In the Land Tax return for Swanland of 1797, Thomas Beilby is assessed "for House and Mill" at £1, with a rate of four shillings in the pound: so Swanland Mill must have been in existence in or before 1797. Beilby disposed of land to raise capital for the building of the mill.

ROADS

Early Developments

The development of roads in and around Swanland can be traced back to the middle ages. Up to the beginning of the fourteenth century there was no consecrated ground for burials in Hull, and funeral parties had to travel along the river bank to the 'mother' church at Hessle. In winter months they were at serious risk from the high tides, a situation which so appalled Archbishop Corbridge that, in 1301, he ordered that a graveyard be consecrated near the Holy Trinity Church in Hull.[71]

It was against this background that Inquisitions of 1303 led to proposals for a new forty-foot road leading westward from Hull to join with the King's highway (linking Beverley with Hessle) at Anlaby. The route passed over common pastures between Hull and Anlaby which were shared not only by Myton and Anlaby, but also, perhaps surprisingly, by Ferriby and Swanland to the west. This is one of the earliest references to Swanland in connection with roads. Indeed, for many years there were almost no other routes in the area which merited the description 'roads'.

An Act of 1555 directed that Surveyors of the Highways be appointed for each parish at the annual vestry meeting. In time, these officers became more usually known as Overseers of the Highways and, like the parish's Overseers of the Poor, they had the power to raise a local rate, in this case for the maintenance of roads within the parish boundaries. They were answerable, for the discharge of their duties, to the Justices of the Peace. North Ferriby Church Book[72] records the following names as Overseers for Swanland:

> Robert Coulson and Peter Burrill, appointed on 14 April 1691,
>
> John Turner and John Jefferson Jnr., appointed on 29 March 1692,
>
> Peter Acy and Samuel Newton, appointed on 10 April 1694,
>
> Henry Watson and Benjamin Galland, appointed on 16 March 1695.

Parishes were also required to provide labour for maintenance work, as instanced by the following document:[73]

Justices Order for Statute work 1700.

At a Petty or Special Sessions of the Peace for the said Riding held at the house of Mrs Harrison before John Bowman and Francis Best Esq., two of His Majesty's Justices of the East Riding. It is therefore ordered, and the Justices do adjudge and determine, that the inhabitants and others in the following Parishes, Townships and Districts chargeable to the said Roads shall, within their several and respective Parishes, Townships and Districts, do and perform severally their statute work upon the said Roads this year at such times and places and in such a manner as the surveyors nominated by the Trustees appointed by the said Acts shall order and direct viz. Swanland: 1 day.

The Highways Act of 1773[74] gave JPs the power to take action at the Assizes or Quarter Sessions, on the sworn testimony of a Surveyor of the Highway, against Parishes that failed to maintain their roads, and fines were imposed. Fines were assessed according to labour cost, *e.g.* 1s.6d. for one man's labour, 3s.0d. for a man and a horse, and 10s.0d. for a cart and two men. However, these fines were remitted if it could be shown that subsequently some improvement had been made. If not, then the fines, less certain court fees, would be levied upon two or three parishioners and the money paid over to one of the parish Surveyors of the Highway. A list was compiled, specifying those inhabitants within the townships liable to do statute work on the Highways, according to the rental value of the land and property which they occupied, as the list for Swanland of 1779 (Appendix 3) shows.[75]

The material used for the surface of local roads was usually chalk, as evidenced by the existence of a number of pits, especially along the line of the former northerly extension of Woodgates Lane.

Turnpikes

A turnpike was literally a long pole, operated on a pivoted bar, and used as a barrier to that part of a road controlled by a trust. Such trusts were established by Acts of Parliament for periods of 21 years to oversee the upkeep of important public roads and to collect tolls from the users of such roads. The first gate was set up in 1663 in Cambridgeshire, on the London to York road. By the end of the eighteenth century some 20,000 miles of roads were turnpiked.[76]

In the mid-eighteenth century, as Hull merchants began to build themselves new houses outside the town, the need for road improvements became urgent. Travellers between Hull and Kirkella (and probably to Swanland) often had to make a three or four mile detour because the road was impassable.[77] Daily travellers to Hull therefore welcomed the advent of the turnpike roads. In 1765 the Beverley to Hessle road was turnpiked, as was the Kirkella to North Cave, via Raywell, in 1774. Charles Frost, a Hull solicitor and historian, campaigned vigorously for a turnpiked road from Hull to Ferriby. He found some opposition from Hull Corporation thought to have been due to objections raised earlier by Henry Broadley and Henry Sykes over Enclosure at Swanland and Ferriby. The Hull-Anlaby Kirkella Turnpike Trust, fearing competition, was also opposed to it.

The Ferriby Turnpike was eventually introduced on 28 July 1825[78] and continued as such until 1873. The road ran from Love Lane in Hull, near the junction of Waverley Street and Cogan Street, along the line of Hessle Road to Hessle. From Hessle the route proceeded northwards along the Beverley road as far as Anlaby and thence to Swanland and on to Ferriby.

It is noted that in 1834 the road material was gravel obtained from the seashore and the requirement was 650 tons per year. The receipts in tolls rose from £97.17.4. in 1826-27 to £345 in 1831-32. In 1827-28 the surveyors of the Highways for the Township of Ferriby paid £18 towards the cost of the trust, compared with Hessle's payment of £90 and Swanland's £26.13.11.[79]

Tolls

Examples of Tolls:

	Hull to Beverley 1744	Hull to Kirkella 1745
Coach drawn by 6 horses	1/6	1/=
Coach drawn by 3 or 4 horses	1/=	8d
Coach drawn by 2 horses	9d	6d
Coach drawn by one horse	6d	3d
Wagon drawn by 5 or more horses	1/6	1/=
Wagon drawn by 3 or 4 horses	1/=	8d
Wagon drawn by 2 horses	9d	6d
Wagon drawn by 1 horse	6d	3d
Each horse laden or unladen	1½d	1d
Calves, pigs etc per score	5d	5d

No tolls were taken on Election days, or from people travelling to and from Church or Chapel on Sundays, or soldiers on the march, pedestrians, vagrants with legal passes, ploughs, barrows, implements of husbandry, or carts carrying manure or road repair materials. A composition of tolls for a period [a kind of 'season ticket'] could be arranged by the trustees for regular users. Tolls were usually taken once a day within a period midnight to midnight and sometimes tolls were interchangeable.[80]

Roads in Swanland before and after the Enclosure Act

The Parliamentary Enclosure Acts of the eighteenth and early nineteenth centuries brought about the consolidation of local landholdings, replacing multiple holdings of narrow strips within the open field system by allocations of larger plots. Each holder was responsible for suitably enclosing the land allocated to him while, at the same time, agreed provision was made for better drainage and new roads. A Bill for Enclosure could only succeed if supported by the owners of at least 75% of the land concerned, and no real progress towards implementing the enclosure of lands in Swanland was made until the 1820s.

The Commissioners responsible for implementing the scheme were required to define the public rights of way including roads, bridleways and footpaths. Some of the roads followed the lines of ancient highways but others were new routes across the former open fields and common pasture. Roads were to be of standard widths, usually thirty or forty foot.[81]

Reference to contemporary and modern maps shows that, within the township of Swanland, several of the present roads pre-date the Enclosure Act. Those we now know as Main Street, West End, Woodgates Lane, West Leys Road, Kemp Road, Tranby Lane and Melton Bottom. As a consequence of the Act, several new roads were constructed. These included: the one which is now Mill Road and Mill Hill, linking the western end of Swanland to Melton Bottom, and a short road leading northwards from Melton Bottom to land at Raywell occupied by Daniel Sykes[82] (nowadays a largely disused bridleway). The present Dale Road (north of the pinfold – see below) and Occupation Lane were also laid out.[83]

Finally, certain other pre-enclosure roads and paths were "stopped up and discontinued"[84] during the enclosure process. In particular, Woodgates Lane (No.11 on the relevant map[84]), which formerly extended northwards over the fields and across Melton Bottom near its junction with Chalk Lane, was terminated at its junction with Mill Road and Mill Hill, near the present water tower. A narrow bridle path (No.16) linking West Leys Road to Woodgates Lane, along the line of a field boundary on the north side of Gorse Hill, was taken out of use, and a field track known as Gate Gate Trod (No.7), which stretched for over a mile and a half in a south-easterly direction (towards Hesslewood) from the junction of Kemp Road with Tranby Lane, was also stopped up. On the northern side of the village, certain back lanes which ran roughly parallel with West End and Main Street, behind the old enclosures associated with the houses, were incorporated into new farmland enclosures.[62, 83]

Another notable road change which occurred at that time was the realignment of Tranby Lane (No.9[84]) in the vicinity of Swanland Hall, which afforded its occupants greater privacy. A twenty-foot road to the east of the Hall (No.10), linking Main Street with Tranby Lane was also stopped up,[84] possibly for similar reasons.

Further notes on the road system, with twentieth century additions, are given by Wheeler and Wheeler,[85] but the map appended here indicates the major changes brought about by enclosure. The following matters are also of interest.

In the eighteenth century, the road leading northwards from the pond followed the line of the present Dale Road for only about a hundred and fifty yards. At that point, and just to the east of the road, there was a pinfold or small enclosure for the confining of stray animals. This lay immediately to the north of the old enclosures adjoining the dwellings in the main street.[62] The back lanes, which ran east-west behind these old enclosures, also met the road here, at which point the northerly route gave way to two fourteen-foot tracks.

One of these (No.13[84]) veered off to the east, across the North Field, and linked up with the present Westella Road at the point where it now joins Occupation Lane. This section, too, was also known as Westella Road at that time.[86]

The other (No.12[84]) veered west for a short distance, then continued northwards on a course roughly parallel with the present Dale Road but about a hundred yards to the west, finally joining Melton Bottom at its junction with Chalk Lane. Both of these tracks were extinguished in 1829, when the newly laid Dale Road and Occupation Lane had come into use.[84]

Dale Road was at first known locally as Crowther Lane in acknowledgement of land held by the Crowthers in the vicinity.[83] Later on it became Post Office Lane, when the former Post Office was located just a little way up this road. Only in the twentieth century does it appear to have become known by its present name.

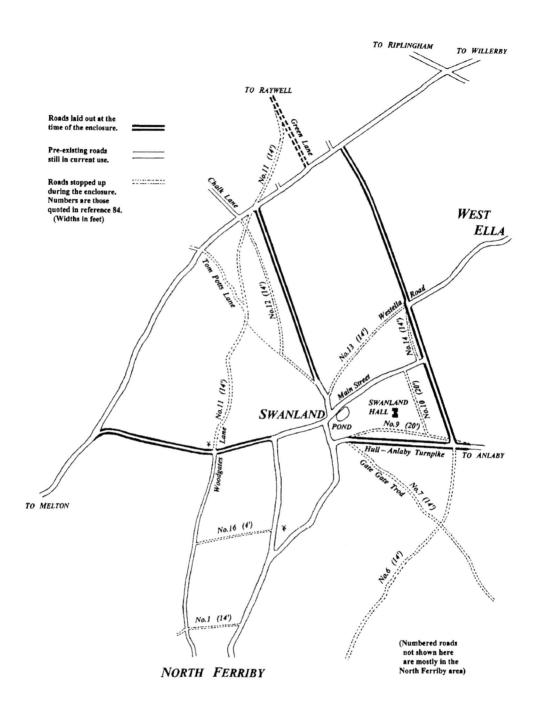

Fig. 11 A Map showing roads in and around Swanland and some eighteenth century roads and tracks stopped up at the time of enclosure

It was on the eastern side of the village, however, that enclosure brought the most radical changes to the road system. Mention has been made already of the stopping up of Gate Gate Trod and the realignment of Tranby Lane in the vicinity of Swanland Hall. By then, of course, Tranby Lane was part of the forty-foot turnpike road linking Anlaby to Swanland and Ferriby. From a point on that road just beyond the present extent of the village, an old road (No.8,[84] not shown in Fig.11) on the south side ran diagonally across the fields to link up with Jenny Brough Lane at its present most westerly right-angle bend. This old road, too, disappeared at the time of the enclosure.

The creation of a straight new north-south route at the eastern end of the village, linking Melton Bottom to Tranby Lane, was a bold development. What now begins as Occupation Lane, continues as Beech Hill Road and finally becomes Greenstiles Lane was a completely new road. Initially the entire length was called Greenstiles Lane, after an old enclosure known as Green Stiles at the northern end, near Melton Bottom. The northern section, now Occupation Lane, was not expected to be as heavily used as the middle and southern sections, now Beech Hill and Greenstiles Lane. It was therefore set out to a width of only twenty-four feet, compared to thirty-six feet elsewhere. Although there had been a road linking Westella Road to Main Street (No.14), it lay slightly to the west of the line of the present Beech Hill Road, and was stopped up once the new road was established. Again, the former road linking Main Street to Tranby Lane (No.10) lay somewhat to the west of the present Greenstiles Lane, nearer to Swanland Hall and, as already mentioned, this too was stopped up. The present Greenstiles Lane lies roughly on the line of the former Town End Balk.

From the south side of Tranby Lane, opposite its junction with Greenstiles Lane, another ancient track (No.6) extended, first south then south-west, for a mile and a quarter, eventually joining Blaskett Lane at Ferriby. Since Blaskett Pond was formerly used as a sheep dip, it may be that this was essentially a sheep track. Be that as it may, it was yet another route that was discontinued after enclosure.

Recently, there has been some local discussion as to whether there was at one time an old road continuing east in line with Main Street and on into Westella. Examination of the enclosure maps shows that this was not so much a road as a water course, namely Easenby Drain, though no doubt a customary track or footpath ran beside it.

References for the Eighteenth Century

1. E Gillett and K A MacMahon, *A History of Hull*
                          (Hull University Press, Second Edition 1989), pp. 206-7

2. Window Tax, Hull City Archives CT102-140

3. Hearth Tax, Lady Day 1672, Public Record Office E179/205/504

4. J G Patton, *A Country Independent Chapel* (A Brown & Sons 1943), pp.28-9

5. T Blossom, *The Life of Mr T Blossom* (a transcript, dated 1895, of Blossom's 1847 autobiographical manuscript) in *Local Notes, Vol: 2,* by W Richardson, a hand written compilation in Hull Central Library, pp. 113-4

6. G Jackson, *Hull in the Eighteenth Century*, (University of Hull OUP), p.110

7. K J Allison, *Hull Gent Seeks Country Residence*,
                          (East Yorkshire Local History Society 1981), p.43

8. International Genealogical Index

9. a) Barnard *Hull Poll Books as Directories*, (1747)   (Local History Unit, Hull College), p.7

    b) Burial Register 1689 to 1792, Holy Trinity, Hull.

10. Hull City Archives TLA 3063/15

11. Hull City Archives BRN 614 (M837)

12. Hull City Archives DMT 4/431   /440

13. G Hadley, *A History of Hull* (T Briggs, Hull 1788), p.345

14. *ibid.* p.348

15. P Roebuck, *Yorkshire Baronets 1640-1760*, (University of Hull OUP, 1980) p.27

16. J Tickell, *A History of the Town and County of Kingston-upon-Hull*, p.863

17. Baptismal Register 1689 to 1782, Holy Trinity, Hull

18. *Land Tax Returns 1791,* Hull City Archives DMX 268/29

19. East Riding Registry of Deeds DDJA 67/2

20. Burke's Peerage and Baronetage (106th Edition, 1999), p.2919

21. W Sykes from the manuscripts of J Richardson, *History of the Streets of Hull,* (reprinted 1980 by the Malet Lambert High School from a 1915 reprint in the Hull and East Yorkshire Times), p.11

22. East Riding Registry of Deeds DC620

23. East Riding Registry of Deeds EL311 371

24. S Dalby, *The Todds of Swanland* (2001)

25. *Dictionary of National Biography* (Compact Edition), p.2940

26. *Hull Daily Mail* 5th July 1980

27. J and C A Wheeler, *Swanland: Recollections of Village Life*
(Wheeler & Wheeler 1984),   pp.19-32

28. D Chapman-Huston, *Sir James Reckitt – A Memoir*, (Faber & Gwyer 1924), p.203

29. J G Patton, *op.cit.,* p.29

30. J G Patton, *ibid.,* p.60

31. J and C A Wheeler, *op.cit.,* p.29

32. *Land Tax Returns* 1797, DMX 268/46

33. D E Ginter, *A Measure of Wealth:* the English Land Tax in Historical Analysis (1992)

34. J G Patton, *op.cit.* p.34

35. T Blossom, *op.cit.* pp.82-233

36. T Blossom, *ibid.* p.83

37. T Blossom, *ibid.* p.85

38. T Blossom, *ibid.* pp.93-95

39. T Blossom, *ibid.* p.105

40. T Blossom, *ibid.* pp.105-107

41. T Blossom, *ibid.* p.109

42. T Blossom, *ibid.* p.111

43. T Blossom, *ibid.* p.111-123

44. J G Patton, *op.cit.,* p.37

45. T Blossom, *op.cit.* pp.123-127

46. Militia Act 1757 (30 Geo.II c25)

47. T Blossom, *op.cit.* p.127

48. T Blossom, *op.cit.* pp.127-145

49. T Blossom, *ibid.* pp.141, 145

50. T Blossom, *ibid.* p.145

51. T Blossom, *Ibid.* p.149

52. T Hiney, *On The Missionary Trail* (Vintage 2000), p.38
    [NB This author confuses Blossom with his colleague, Armitage, and describes Blossom as a weaver rather than a joiner.]

53. T Blossom, *op.cit.* p.171

54. T Blossom, *ibid.* p.177

55. T Blossom, *ibid.* p.181

56. T Blossom, *ibid.* pp.175-191

57. T Blossom, *ibid.* p.191

58. T Blossom, *ibid.* p.223

59. T Blossom, *ibid.* pp.225-229

60. J Crowther, *Enclosure Commissioners and Surveyors of the East Riding*
    (East Yorkshire Local History Society 1986), p.7

61. D Hey [Ed.], *The Oxford Companion to Local and Family History*
    (Oxford University Press 1966), p.32

62. Pre-enclosure (1824) Map of Swanland
    East Riding Registry of Deeds, DDX/25/5 (also DX/28)

63. D Hey [Ed.], *op.cit.* p.395

64. D Hey [Ed.], *ibid.* p.213

65. D Hey [Ed.], *ibid.* p.234

66. A Harris, The Open Fields of East Yorkshire
    (East Yorkshire Local History Society 1959), p.10

67. A Harris, *ibid.* p.19

68. K E Laister, *The Farms of North Ferriby*, (Humberside Christian Press, 1997)

69. T Jefferys, *The County of York, Published according to Act of Parliament
    25 March 1772 by T Jefferys*, [112¾ × 91 inches] (Second Edition 1775)

70. C Greenwood, *Map of the County of York, surveyed in the years 1815 to 1817
    by C Greenwood, Wakefield, 4 June 1817* [nine sheets, each 27¼ × 23 inches]

71. E Gillett and K A MacMahon, *op.cit.* p.7

72. D J Bulman and A Eastcrabbe [Eds.] *North Ferriby: A Villagers' History*
(Lockington Publishing Company 1982), p.48

73. East Riding Registry of Deeds DDBD 84/3

74. Highways Act 1773 (13 Geo.III c78)

75. East Riding Registry of Deeds DDBD 70/1

76. G Hindley, *A History of Roads* (Citadel Press 1972), p.61

77. E Gillett and K A MacMahon, *op.cit.* p.234

78. 6 Geo.IV c152

79. D J Bulman and A Eastcrabbe [Eds.] *op.cit.* p.82

80. K A MacMahon, *Roads and Turnpike Trusts in Eastern Yorkshire*
(East Yorkshire Local History Society), p.47

81. D Hey [Ed.], *op.cit.* p.154

82. Public Notice, *The Hull Advertiser,* 14 January 1825

83. Enclosure Award (1837) Map IA/115, East Riding of Yorkshire Archives

84. Order and map (1829) for the closure of old roads and tracks in and around
the township of Swanland as required by the Enclosure Commissioners,
HD/34 East Riding of Yorkshire Archives

85. J and C A Wheeler, *op.cit.* pp.10-12

86. Indenture dated 6th April 1825 for the sale of land by Samuel Shaw of Brantingham
to Nathaniel Shaw of Swanland, Hull City Archives DMS6 Box 394

THE NINETEENTH CENTURY

INTRODUCTION

> *Of all situations for a constant residence*
> *that which appears to me the most delightful*
> *is a little village far in the country............*
> *with inhabitants whose faces are familiar*
> *to us as the flowers of our garden......*
> *where we know everyone, are known to*
> *everyone,...and hope that everyone feels*
> *an interest to us.*
>
> *Our Village   Mary Russell Mitford, 1824*

The purpose of the following chapter is to try to paint a picture of the village at the beginning of the nineteenth century, to see how it develops as the century progresses, and to follow the occupations of the villagers. For some of the better documented families, a little of their family history is provided, with the occasional anecdote.

Whilst for many life in the nineteenth century was a time of dramatic change, the turbulence of the period largely passed by the quiet village of Swanland. In nearby Kingston-upon Hull, the population increased from 29,000 in 1801 to 255,000 by the end of the century. In Swanland it remained essentially static.

That is not to say there were no changes in the village: there were. Swanland's fields were enclosed along with those of Ferriby, Kirkella, and Willerby, by the Inclosure* Act of 1824, reflecting the need to provide food for the growing populations of the towns. Mechanical drills, reapers and threshing machines appeared on its farms. Industrialists came to live in the village, preferring its relatively healthy environment and beautiful location to the smoke and smells of the town. They purchased land in and around the village.

Communications improved. Thomas Fillingham's horse drawn omnibus was established in the village in 1831 and claimed to be "the oldest conveyance between Hull, Anlaby, Kirkella, and Swanland". From 1840, the Hull and Selby Railway opened at North Ferriby for passengers and parcels. The village school, run by the Independent Chapel, came under Government Inspection in 1871, and by the end of the century an element of local democracy had been introduced into village affairs through the establishment of the Parish Council.

Despite such changes, Swanland remained a quiet agricultural community throughout the nineteenth century, and was largely self-sufficient. It was centred on its dozen or so farms, which were supported by the traditional craftsmen and farm workers living in the village. What follows is the story of that community, and of a way of life long past.

* *"Inclosure": the spelling for enclosure at the time.*

THE VILLAGE AT THE START OF THE CENTURY

At the beginning of the nineteenth century, Swanland was a community of some 418 souls. [1] By 1840 this had risen to 478. The township comprised "...nearly 3000 acres of land, including many scattered farms on the eastern side of the wolds, part of Dairy Cotes,..and the estate of Braffords Hall, a handsome mansion house of white brick, at the head of a romantic dell."

Braffords, (Raywell), Wold Ings, (Dairy Cotes), and Wold Carr, (Newington), formed detached parts of the administrative township of Swanland, dating from medieval times. [2]

The village can perhaps best be seen by reference to the Pre Enclosure Map of 1824, (Fig 12). Most of the ninety or so houses in the main village ran linearly along Main Street and West End. A back road, which no longer exists, ran behind them to the north. The chalk forming this road was recently uncovered during preparation for the Sykes Close development.

Following the map through from east to west, we can form an idea of what the village looked like. At the edge of the village, to the south-east, lay the eighteenth century Hall, which at that time was Swanland's only major house. In 1818 it was occupied by Nicholas Sykes. [3] Priory Farm, and Dam Farm, (Mere House) lay along Main Street, as did the properties which were later to become known as Dower House and Toft House. Dam farm, did not have the impressive Tudor façade which its successor, Mere House, was to have. [4] The Independent Chapel, which overlooked the pond had been rebuilt in 1803.

Cottages stood at the eastern end of *West End,* which on some maps appears as Town Street. One of these, the present Post Office, is dated 1721. The eastern end of the *Old Parsonage,* built in 1696, was of only one storey, and of red brick. A stable for the parson's horse lay at the west end of the garden.

By 1797 Swanland already had its own mill. [5] It stood at the highest point in the village at the junction of Woodgates Lane and the road now called Mill Road. Although it does not appear on the Pre Enclosure Map of 1824, it is clearly shown on Greenwood's map of 1817. Ferriby Mill, an old post mill, is situated close to where Kemp Road and West Leys Road meet.

The Parliamentary Enclosure of Swanland had yet to come, and surrounding the village lay great open fields, with their cultivated strips.

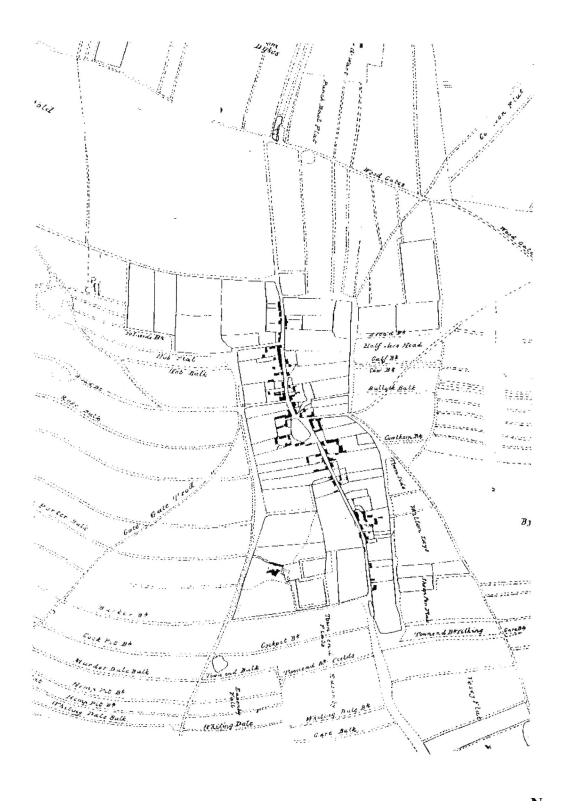

Fig.12 Pre Enclosure Map

42

The township was already linked to the neighbouring villages of Ferriby, Tranby, and Westella, [6] and to the route from Willerby to Melton via Woodgates Lane and Tom Potts Road. From the Willerby to Melton road it was possible to access the North Cave Turnpike. It would have to wait for the enclosures of 1824 onwards to enjoy the additional roadways connecting Mill Road to Melton, and Greenstiles Occupation Lane to Swanland Dale.

We must not close this snapshot of the village at the beginning of the century, without remarking on the views for which it was so noted. Let us take Baines' commentary of 1823, as an example:

> "The landscapes seen from this village," he says, "are greatly admired
> by visitors for their beauty, variety, and grandeur. An elevated spot near
> Swanland Mill, commands a view of the Trent and the country adjacent,
> The whole course of the Humber down to Spurn lights.."[8]

THE CHANGING SCENE

Swanland remained a small agricultural community throughout the nineteenth century. There were 102 houses in 1891 compared with the 96 of 1841,[9] and the population peaked in 1871 at 517. [10] Nevertheless there were changes in the village, and one of these, enclosure, was dramatic.

The Fields

In 1826 Robert Sharp wrote in his diary:

> "The last time I was at Ferriby I saw what may be called the first fruits of Inclosure, viz. a Board put up with a notice that any person trespassing on the land would be prosecuted. No walking in the field now, but dust to gratify the weary traveller."[11]

What a change this must have produced on the landscape. Hitherto there had been the great open fields divided into strips, as we saw in the previous chapter, with an owner's land holdings widely spread. The open fields were now divided by fencing and hedging, forming smaller enclosures centred on the farmsteads. The process increased the acreage available for ploughing by dispensing with the balks, brought land holdings together, was more amenable to the use of machinery, and allowed intensive livestock farming. It had been a necessary response to the increase in population.

Swanland already had some ancient enclosures surrounding its houses, and in certain of its open fields, but on the 3 June 1824, later then for most villages in the area, an act of Parliament was passed entitled *An Act for Inclosing Lands in the townships of Ferriby, Swanland, Kirk Ella, West-Ella, and Willerby*. This resulted in enclosure of all the fields. The awards made were listed and identified on the Enclosure Map of 1837, (Fig13). Two examples have been extracted from this large document.[12]

The first relates to John Crowther:

> "..Also we have divided set out and do award unto and for John Crowther of Swanland aforesaid yeoman….that piece of Land numbered 83…containing one rood and five perches..bounded on the south by an ancient enclosure"

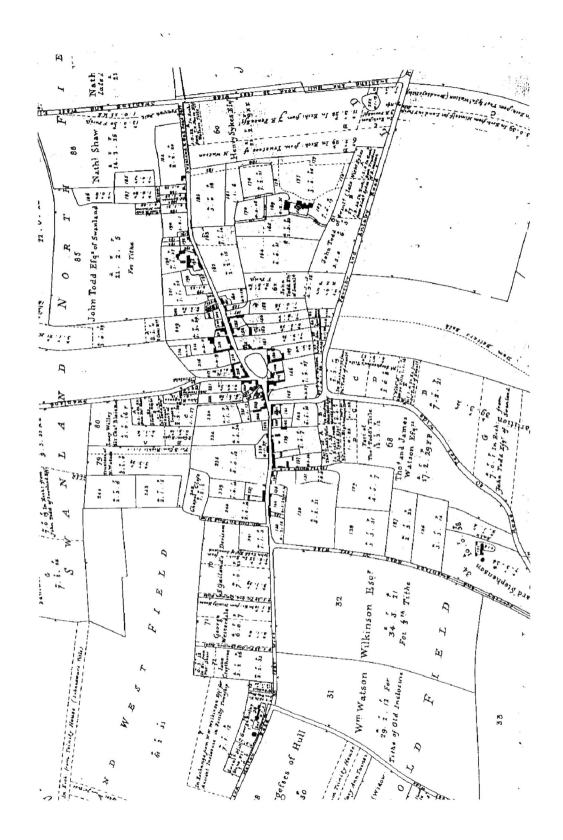

Fig.13   Enclosure Map 1837

45

Dale Road was initially named Crowther Lane after this family. More recently Crowther Way has retained the association.

The second example relates to land owned by the Watson family, on which James was subsequently to build his *Manor House*. It illustrates how land holdings were brought together. Thomas and James Watson were the sons of Thomas and Ann Watson of Wauldby. They were rich farmers. In 1837, they already held: "..an ancient enclosure numbered 129 [on the enclosure Map], situated between West Leys Road, (then called Ferriby & Swanland Road), and Kemp Road (then Ferriby & Anlaby Road)."It may have been the four-acre plot off what is now West Leys Road, conveyed to Henry Watson by Christophcr Bacon in 1705.[13]

By reference to the Enclosure Map we can see how the Commissioners built on this original holding to bring the Watsons' land together. Adjacent plots were awarded to them in exchange for rights elsewhere. Allotments included:

Allotment No.	Acre	Award Rood	Perch	Basis of Award.
68	17	2	29	
68	13	3	12	Part of Todd's Title..in lieu or compensation for certain lands, rights of stray, and other rights in and over the said open fields in the parish of Ferriby.
A				In exchange from John Todd
B				In exchange from John Todd for old inclosures.
C				Part of Kemp's Title
D	1	3	0	In lieu of compensation for the rights of common and other rights belonging to three ancient messuages, cottages, and dwelling houses situate in the parish of Ferriby.
69	0	1	2	Etc.

Was enclosure successful? Did it increase productivity? Nationally the answer to both these questions was yes. The amount of land under cultivation increased by between 100 and 150 per cent.[14] But Swanland's Nathaniel Shaw saw things differently:

> "There has not been a good crop in Swanland Field since the enclosure,"he writes. "Before that time it was noted for its fine crops of wheat. The last year there was not more than five loads in four acres, but this was not the worst. For in the open state the land was 15s per acre with the privilege of 500 acres of common land for no rent. But now the rent is from 50 to 55s, so that this improving ..is growing worse."[15]

Although no reference can be found on the effect of enclosure on smallholders in the village, in general they faired poorly. Some could not afford the cost of enclosure, and common grazing land was lost. Some small farmers became farm labourers, or moved to work in the towns. The larger landowner benefited.

Tithes

The upkeep of the Incumbent of a parish church was originally maintained through tithes. These were a tenth part of a village's income, calculated on produce, stock, or labour. Ownership of tithes became more complicated after the Reformation, when monastic holdings were taken over by the Crown and passed on to laymen.

In Swanland, allotments of land in lieu of tithes were made at the time of the enclosures. One such was an allotment to John Todd Esq., (Fig 13, Allotment No 85), but the system continued in detached parts of the township until 1840. Then, under the Tithe Commutation Act of 1836, all remaining tithes were commuted to rent.

Records of "Ancient Inclosure in the Township of Swanland subject to Tithe - 1840",[16] include references to the Humber Bank Brick Yard, York Grounds, Dairy Cotes, Braffords [Hall], Part of the Hull and Selby Railway, and Newington.

Landowners, occupiers and tithe owners are listed, together with the rent charges payable by the landowners or tenants in lieu of tithes. These were payable as follows:

	£	s	d
To John Ringrose [of Cottingham]	115	0	0
To William Duesbury [of Beverley]	15	0	0
To Joseph Sykes [of Kirkella]	12	12	12
	142	12	12

The sum of £12. 4. 2 was payable as a fixed payment under the Swanland Inclosure Act to the Vicar of Kirkella… "in lieu of tithe of Wool and Lamb and other small vicarial tithes…"

At the time, "…the whole Township of Swanland …containe[d] by estimation 3,200 acres", and "..the whole quantity of the lands which [were] subject to the payment of any kind of tithes [was]…601 acres." There was no common land subject to tithes.

2,598 acres were exempt from payment of tithe…by virtue of the Swanland Inclosure Act, land having been awarded to the tithe holders in lieu. By making such awards at the time of Inclosure rather than tithe commutation, the village of Swanland was not included in a Tithe Map. From a historian's point of view this is a loss as the Tithe Map numbers every parcel of land and every building, and from the accompanying apportionment the owner and occupier can be discovered.

New Houses

Before looking in detail at the new building of the period it is useful to form a general impression of change. As we saw earlier the number of houses in the village did not increase significantly during the nineteenth century. Three large houses appeared, however, built for Swanland's gentry, and Mere House appears to have been rebuilt in its present Tudor style between 1839 and 1855. Towards the end of the century "model farms" were to be seen.

The Independent Chapel was rebuilt in 1803, and a chapel for Primitive Methodists constructed in 1828. In 1855 the east end of The Old Parsonage was rebuilt two storeys high. There was no Anglican building until 1899. The schoolroom associated with the Independent Chapel was rebuilt in the middle of the century, and a new school provided by John Todd of The Hall in 1876.

We can now look at some of these changes in more detail.

Mere House (See Cover Page)

*Mere House, Main Street. Mid-Victorian red
brick house with stone hoodmoulds to windows.
Tudor style, of two storeys…..*

*Pevsner & Neave
The Building of England,
York & the East Riding*

Reference to the deeds of Mere House indicate that in 1839 it bore the name *Dam Farm.*[17] It was at that time in the ownership of Sarah Osborne, widow of a former Recorder of Hull. Sarah sold the house that year to William Walmsley, a solicitor, who had lived in Parliament Street in the city, but by 1841 had come to live in Swanland.

The Pre Enclosure Map of 1824 and the Enclosure Map of 1837 both show buildings on the site having the appearance of a farmstead, with a fold yard and barn, (still standing), on the northern side. The present shape of the building was not shown until the Ordnance Survey Map of 1855. Since a shield above the entrance to the present house bears the letters W.W. it would seem that somewhere between 1839 and 1855, William Walmsley rebuilt the house in Tudor style, setting its centre section well back from the street. The two wings of the house were largely retained but were refaced with new bricks. Corbels were included in the brickwork of the building. Those in the string course of the upper storey have in the past resulted in the house being called Monkey Hall. The reputation of the house as one of the oldest in the village doubtless stems from its Tudor appearance.

A younger Walmsley, William Henry, (landed proprietor), succeeded the first as occupier of the house, although he never owned the property. At the time of the 1851 Census he had five children, three visitors and five servants in the house. He died in 1887.

James Walmsley, who never lived there, eventually sold Mere House in 1881.

The names of some of the later occupiers of the house are available from Census Returns. In 1881 two Scottish ladies, a Maria Hill and her sister lived there. By 1891 a Russian merchant, Reginald Corrie, occupied the property, together with his six children, sister-in-law, and three servants.

We know most about the house from the Finance (1909-1910) Act, in which property details were listed as a basis for taxation. Sir James Reckitt then owned the house. Patton suggests that his sister-in-law, Mrs Houghton may have lived there for a time. The tenant in 1910 was Percy Westerdale, a farmer. The house came with three-quarters of an acre of land and included dining room, drawing room, smoke room, kitchen, sitting room, and six bedrooms. A trap house, saddle room and stable were associated with the building.

The Manor House c1848

In about 1848, a most impressive new house was built for a rich farmer who until then had lived and farmed at Wauldby. It was built on his own land in Swanland, between West Leys Road and Kemp Road.[18] We have already come across the gentleman in question when considering enclosure, for the house was built for James Watson.

There are numerous anecdotes relating to his reasons for building it. James and Thomas Watson, although holding land in their own right, were also tenants of the Broadleys, who owned the six hundred acres the Watsons farmed at Wauldby.[19] The farmhouse they occupied there had been rebuilt in 1839, but James felt that he merited something better. There was a difference of opinion. Mr Broadley thought that the existing farmhouse was: "quite good enough for a farmer".[20] James responded that he: "could build himself a house as good as Broadley any day". Thus the grand house at Swanland came to be built.

The reason for it being called The Manor House remains uncertain. A previous historian, Major Desmond Chapman-Huston, believed that it was because in 1695 a John Parker, Lord of the Manor of Swanland and Ferriby, had built a Manor House nearby which his great-great-grandson, Samuel Parker Watson had demolished.[21] The present study has not found corroborative evidence for this hypothesis, but nor has it been possible to disprove it. No earlier Manor House shows on the Enclosure Map of 1837, but then it could well have been demolished by that time. It is perhaps of some interest that James Watson's earlier house at Wauldby was called The Manor House. Did he simply carry this name forward when he moved to his new residence in Swanland?

Whatever the reason, photographs show that it was certainly a fine house, (Figs 14 & 15). We are told that:

> "..at the time a mansion belonging to the first Duke of Sutherland was being demolished, and the architect…purchased from his Grace all the mahogany doors and frames, as well as the mantelpieces for hall, morning room, and drawing room,…a glass chandelier which had cost the Duke of Sutherland five hundred pounds,..and the staircase." [22]

It is said that at the time the Manor was built its owner disliked the appearance of the nearby Ferriby Mill, and a belt of trees was planted round the land on which it stood. The hope was that these would grow up and keep the wind off the mill's sails.[23] The trees can be seen on the Ordnance Survey Map of 1855.

James Watson died in 1855 aged 63, so he did not live long in The Manor. He was succeeded by Robert Brough, a farmer from Melton, who took the name Watson to become Robert Brough Watson.

Robert married a Miss Davenport, and on his death in 1879, The Manor House passed to a John Davenport. It came as: "…a great surprise to him and his family."[24] In 1884 it was purchased by Sir James Reckitt, and by 1901 had become known as Swanland Manor. Both John Davenport, and Sir James Reckitt were Lords of the Manor of Swanland.[25,26]

During Robert Brough Watson's time at The Manor, he purchased Ferriby Mill, and provided a cricket ground on the grass land that belonged to it.[27]

When James Reckitt took over the property considerable alterations were made. A billiard room was added to the house (Fig.15), the gardens were considerably enlarged, and a model farm was built.[28] The house contained a fine collection of paintings, including works by Turner, Frith, Birkett Foster, Leader and Herring.[29]

Fig.14   Swanland Manor East Front

Fig.15   The Billiard Room, Swanland Manor

Rock Lodge & Rose Cottage (prior to 1860s) and Swanland House (1860s)

During the first half of the century, a retired merchant, Charles Thompson and his daughter, Miss Jane Thompson, occupied what appears to have been a very pretty little estate, essentially on the site of the present Swanland House.[30] The estate comprised mansion, stables, paddock, plantation, meadow, orchard, and kitchen garden in all about 8 acres, and included terracing, fish ponds, and summer houses. Immediately to the west lay Rose Cottage, occupied in 1841 by a builder, Francis Richards.[31] Both appear on the Ordnance Survey Map of 1855.

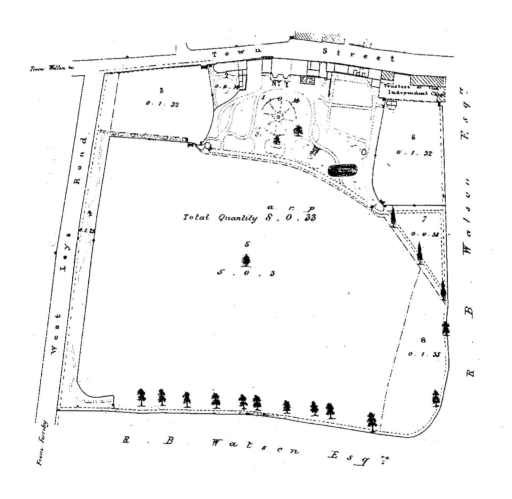

Fig.16 Rock Lodge and Grounds 1861

In 1859 Miss Thompson died, and by 1871 Rock Lodge had been replaced by Swanland House, built: "just to the south of the old site."[32] Swanland House, a fine example of Victorian architecture is now a listed building. From 1871 until his death in 1893, it was occupied by Andrew Duncan, owner of a seed crushing mill. He was doubtless seeking refuge from the dark and dingy neighbourhoods of Hull in which his mill stood and where: "..bone mills, blubber yards, tanneries and tar sheds gave out their two and seventy various stinks, all perfect and well defined."[33]

Northfield House

In 1825 Robert Sharp wrote in his diary: "Nathaniel Shaw has built a new house in Swanland Field, between there and Westella". The "new house" was Northfield House, now Beech Hill, and it duly appeared on the Ordnance Survey Map of 1855. In 1869 the property was sold by auction, the bill of sale describing it as: "A Mansion called Northfield House, with Plantation, Pleasure Grounds, Lawn, Yards and Garden, Lodge and Cottages."[34] It then had with it 75 acres of rich grass land, and was in the occupation of Henry Barkworth (Fig 17).

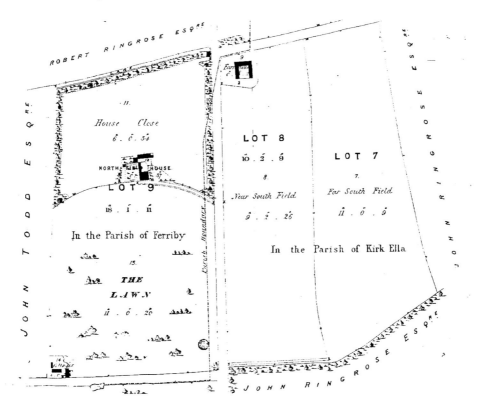

Fig. 17 Plan of Northfield House and Grounds 1869

The Model Farm

The 1850s and 1860s were known as the golden age of Victorian farming. Farming was at last doing well and landowners had capital to invest. "Model Farms" began to appear. In place of the confused farm building of the past, stone and brick buildings came to be built around interlocking yards, with animals and produce sheltered from the weather. Large granaries were often sited to the north or east to provide protection from winter winds.

Swanland has an example, Westfield farm. This initially belonged to Christopher Ringrose, although George Heron farmed it at the time. A sales poster from 1895 describes it as having: "..every accommodation that could be required in a model farmstead", (Fig 18).

SWANLAND

In the East-Riding of the County of York, containing **200 acres**, or thereabouts, known as

"WESTFIELD FARM,"

WITH THE

CAPITAL (RECENTLY ERECTED) RESIDENCE

AND RANGE OF MODERN AND SUBSTANTIAL

FARM BUILDINGS,

Comprising---Stabling, Coach House, Beast, Cow, Calf, Turnip, Cake, Hen and Copper Houses, Large Barn, Granary, Waggon Shed, Implement House, and other Buildings,

TWO LARGE FOLD YARDS,

and every accommodation required in a model Farmstead.

The LAND is in a high and productive state of cultivation, and the RESIDENCE AND FARM BUILDINGS are replete with every convenience.

The Estate is in close proximity to the best residential ones in this part of the country—is of high elevation—and commands extensive and picturesque views of the surrounding country, the Lincolnshire and Yorkshire Wolds and the River Humber.

W. N. LEWENDON & SON

WILL SELL THE ABOVE-MENTIONED VALUABLE ESTATE

BY AUCTION,

Fig. 18   Westfield Farm Notice of Sale 1895

The Chapels, School Room and Old Parsonage

The history of the church and education in the village justify chapters to themselves, which are included elsewhere. Mention is made of them here principally to outline nineteenth century developments.

Since the Toleration Act of 1689, Swanland had been a centre of non-conformist worship for the surrounding area. In 1694 an Independent Chapel and school had been built for: "...the towns of Swanland, Anlaby, Hessle, Kirkella, Willerby, Ferriby, Melton, and Elloughton".[35] At the start of the nineteenth century, however, a new chapel was erected. It was situated on the site of the earlier building, [36] and still stands by the pond today, as the central section of Christ Church.

In 1840, porches were added at the sole cost of John Todd of Tranby Park, and in 1854 the present wings of the chapel were built, paid for by James Watson of the Manor House.[37] The northern wing replaced the original schoolroom and vestry, which had been housed in a cottage-like building. The upper storey had formed the schoolroom, the lower storey the vestry.

Until 1899 the only other church building in Swanland was the Primitive Methodist Chapel, which had been built in 1828 to the north of Main Street on land provided by Henry Sykes. The Religious Census of 1851 does, however, indicate that in that year Wesleyan Methodists were worshipping in the village, in a hired room. In 1899 the first Anglican Church was erected.

Fig.19 The Independent Chapel

The village's schooling in the nineteenth century was largely managed by the Independent Chapel, and in 1876 a new Day and Sunday School were opened: "the Gift of John Todd Esq. of Swanland Hall."

A house for the Minister of the Chapel had been built in 1696,[38] (The Old Parsonage). The east end was only one storey high, and in 1855 it was pulled down and rebuilt two storeys in height in white brickwork. [38] The west end of the parsonage was of red brick. The parsonage had with it a stable that has since been demolished.

Fig. 20   The Old School (left) built in 1876

Ferriby and Swanland Mills

Before Swanland had its own facility, use was made of the post mill belonging to the parish of North Ferriby, located at the junction of West Leys and Kemp Road. This is discussed in the Chapter covering the eighteenth century.

Post mills were followed by smock mills made of wood and were often octagonal, after which came the tower mill built of brick or stone and circular in cross section.[39] From 1797 Swanland had its own mill, which was first owned by Thomas Beilby.[40] We have no indication of the appearance of that first mill, but we know that when it was rebuilt in 1849, (see below), it was a seven storied tower mill, (Fig.21). The precise location of the mill is shown on the enclosure map of 1837 (IA/115) and the road closure map of 1829 (HD/34). Both show the tower of Swanland Mill at the *western* end of the mill yard, next to a stone pit opposite the present water tower. In the London Gazette of 7 February 1834 Thomas Beilby the Elder of Swanland was declared bankrupt. A second mill was built in 1849 at great cost.[41] On the Ordnance Survey Map of 1855, this is clearly shown at the *eastern* end of the yard opposite the present Woodgates Lane.

Fig. 21 Swanland Mill

The 1849 mill was offered for sale in April and September 1860, and again in March 1896. The bill of sale in September 1860 offered:

> "..that valuable brick built corn mill, with the commodious dwelling house messuage, granary, barn, stables and outbuildings, ..and the large garden thereto adjoining,..the dwelling house contain[ing] ..seven rooms, two kitchens and dairy..The mill built in 1849 at great cost [was] seven storeys high and contain[ed] four pairs of stones, cylinder, screen, and other modern machinery."[42]

Towards the end of the century windmills began to be replaced by steam powered roller mills, exemplified by Rank's *Clarence Mill* on the banks of the River Hull. Problems for Swanland's mill were compounded by gale damage. The last tenant, Mr T. Clayton, saw: "various sections of the fan blown clean out, some flying great distances, and being found three miles away." In a further storm a sail was smashed and for a time the mill ran on two sails. The final blow came in 1895 when the main driving shaft was damaged and the mill ceased to work. [41] In 1906 the then derelict mill was demolished by Mr Louis Calvert.

A few lines from *The Miller,* in 1909, provide its epitaph:

> "Swanland Mill which was a famous landmark, has gone to join the rest of the great army of mills that have vanished from this county. It has been demolished down to a low level, and the lower part of it is now made into a workshop for the production of rustic furniture."[43]

VILLAGE OCCUPATIONS

So far we have seen what the village looked like at the beginning of the century, and how it developed in terms of its fields and buildings as the century progressed. We turn now to the villagers; who they were and what they did. The occupations of the villagers and their names, taken from the Census returns of 1841-1891 as listed in Appendix 4 at the end of this chapter.

The Farmers and Agricultural Workers

> *Only a man harrowing clods*
> *In a slow silent walk*
> *With an old horse that stumbles and*
> *Half asleep as they stalk*
>
> *Thomas Hardy.*

Throughout the nineteenth century Swanland's economy was centred on its farms. These provided work for agricultural labourers and trade for the blacksmiths, wheelwrights, millers, and other village businesses.

The township of Swanland included upwards of a dozen farmsteads. Of these three were situated in the detached hamlets of Braffords, Newington and Dairy Cotes, three bordered on Swanland Dale, and two lay south of the village in Humber Dale and South Field. The remainder stood in or close to the village. We know what some of those in the village were called: farms by the name of Northfield, Easenby, Swanland Hall, The Dower House, Priory, Model and Westfield, (See Appendix). We also know that there were at least three others in Main Street and West End, but their names are now lost in the mists of time.

Census returns show that a quarter or more of Swanland's population lived or worked on these farms. The farmer, his family and farm servants lived on the premises. Other agricultural labourers lived out. At harvest time it was common for the craftsmen, women and children of the village to help in the fields.

The farmers were mostly tenants of local landowners. Of the thirteen principal land proprietors shown on the Enclosure Map of 1837, (Fig 13), only one, Nathaniel Shaw, appears as a farmer in the Census Return of 1841. Where landowners farmed their own land, they generally did so through bailiffs or foremen, who were often termed hinds. The Census Return of 1891 identifies Thomas Boothby, Henry Caley, Henry Billaney, Samuel Dennett, and Edward Cowper, as bailiffs or foremen.

The farms themselves were of greatly differing size and purpose. Some were very small. William Dowson farmed no more than nine acres, sufficient to provide pasture for two or three horses and one or two milking cows which were kept for his own use. John Westerdale farmed fifteen acres. On the other hand in 1861 and 1871, Robert Ringrose farmed five hundred acres, and employed eight men and five boys in addition to his farm servants. His would be a mixed farm. In between lay the majority, which ranged from seventy to three hundred acres. Most farmers kept cows and had a dairy: the name survives in the name of a house on Kemp Road today, *The Old Dairy*, built by James Reckitt as his home farm. Farms also clearly stocked sheep. Swanland had nine shepherds in the village.

Fig. 22 Westfield Farm

Some farmers lived alone, perhaps employing a housekeeper. Others, particularly towards the end of the century, had large families. Henry Caley had a family of ten. Additionally there were the farm servants who lived in. There were up to eight such servants living on the farms in Swanland, in the nineteenth century. These generally included a girl, to help about the house.

Farm servants were hired annually at hiring fairs. Statute hirings: "..were held at all market towns and principal villages in the East Riding on hiring days."[44] They were paid at the end of the year they were hired for, and with money in their pockets, the hiring fair was a time for them to enjoy a week's holiday. Robert Sharp refers to one such day in his diary.

Speaking of the fair at South Cave in November 1826, he writes:

> "A holiday this day being Martinmas Monday a good deal of
> rabble in the town. Few of the Men who have been working
> hard all the year can guide themselves properly when they have
> a little leisure time."[45]

Perhaps their behaviour is understandable since for the remainder of the year their lot was one of hard labour. The farm labourer worked from dawn to dusk six days a week. He forked manure in the farm yard and sheaves in the fields. He carried sixteen stone sacks of wheat from threshing machine to granary. For this labour the men were paid about fourteen shillings a week.[46] Of such was George Brooks whose descendants still reside in the village. Women too were employed on the farms. Tess of the D'Urbervilles, when turnip trimming: "..could not prevent the frozen masses biting her fingers."

The nineteenth century saw the introduction of machinery to farms. Although the scattering of seed by hand continued, sometimes with the assistance of a fiddle drill, increasing use was made of horse drawn mechanical drills. At the turn of the century Thomas Blossom had described his new master as a "..very ingenious and good workman as a joiner etc., and the first man that made a threshing machine in this part of the country," (Swanland.), and by the 1820s use of the threshing machine was common.[47] Robert Sharp writes of the drill and the threshing machine in his diary of 20. October, 1826:

> "..Robinson of Mount Airy, [South Cave], and Mr Shackleton
> have each lately got threshing machines, they are nearly as
> prejudicial to the poor threshers as the Power Looms are to the
> hand weavers. The drill for saving corn is the best invention."

Reliable reaping machines were introduced in the 1850s, although even by the 1890s probably only one farm in a hundred had one. Mechanical binders came along in 1870.

Whilst early in the twentieth century the inventory for the sale of Priory Farm included a steam engine, the motive power for most farm machinery, and for the carting of farm products to mill and market, was still the horse. A two hundred acre farm would employ eight to ten magnificent Shire or Clydesdale horses.

It is to be expected that the introduction of machinery would result in a reduction in the numbers employed on Swanland's farms, and so it appears. The number of agricultural labourers fell from 59 in 1841 to 45 in 1881, and then to 35 in 1891.

The Village Craftsmen

The limited availability of transport in the nineteenth century meant that many villages were essentially self-supporting. The village was home to blacksmiths, wheelwrights, carpenters and millers, whose services supported the farms, builders who provided the housing, tailors and shoemakers who made the villagers' breeches and boots, and butchers and grocers who kept them fed. Reference to the Census Returns, (see Appendix), shows that Swanland had at times as many as three blacksmiths, three wheelwrights, six carpenters, three builders, four tailors, and three shoemakers. As might be expected successive generations of the same family often followed the same trade. What follows is the story of these craftsmen.

The Blacksmith

The village blacksmith provided agricultural machinery, farm implements, the iron tyres for wagon wheels, and the shoes for the horses. There were said to be over a million horses used in agriculture in Victorian times, [48] and within the village people say that: "..there were more 'osses than labourers". This was probably so. In addition to forging new ironware, the smith repaired ploughs, drills, and harrows, and sharpened billhooks, scythes, sickles, and axes.

From 1781, through to 1841 the Westerdale family are recorded as being Swanland's blacksmiths. They may have been in the business earlier. At the end of the century Henry Beilby was the smith. The forge at this time was situated in a cottage at the junction of West End and Kemp Road, (Fig 23).

Fig. 23   The Forge Post 1914

The Wheelwright

Before the coming of the internal combustion engine, and for some time afterwards, farm produce was moved by wagon. Milk was taken to market or the nearest railway station and water to the farm by cart. People and goods were conveyed by the local carrier or horse drawn omnibus. The craftsman who made and repaired the wheels of these vehicles was the wheelwright. The wheelwright also worked on the wooden parts of ploughs, harrows, and other farm machinery. The work was skilful, and required a good knowledge of the many woods involved.

An extract from an account of the work a wheelwright undertook provides us with some idea of the task:

> "Now came the job of fixing spikes into the bush. He set the bush
> securely into a waist high wooden vice, and took the first spoke in
> his hand. With a wooden beetle he tapped it gently into its socket.
> Then he looked at its angle. When [he] was happy with the angle of
> his spokes he took a sledge hammer, lifted it high above his head,
> and drove each spoke home with a resounding thud.
>
> When he loosened the vice, he could lift out a circle of spokes
> firmly fixed to the central bush. He carried it to the yard and laid
> it on the wheelstand. Now he had to make the felloes, the sections
> of the wheel rim cut out of pale grey ash which was free from shakes.
> His first job was to plane them smooth, and then using a pattern, mark
> out the curve. They were adzed and smoothed into shape, mortise holes
> cut for the spoke ends, and dowel holes drilled where half tenons
> overlapped….."[49]

Although there would be earlier craftsmen in the trade, the earliest wheelwright we at present have on record in Swanland is Thomas Marshall, to whom Thomas Blossom was first apprenticed late in the eighteenth century. The first in this line of business in the nineteenth century is William Habbershaw. In 1846, his firm was known as *Habbershaw and Grey*. By 1851 Thomas Andrew and the Andrew family were the village wheelwrights, and remained so until 1892. They continued subsequently as joiners.

There is a useful archive relating to the Andrew family from 1862 onwards.[50] Thomas Andrew's customers extended as far afield as Braffords on the east and Melton on the west. His customers were chiefly the farmers we have met earlier, but also included Richard Kirby the builder, Thomas Marshall the miller, and Andrew Duncan, a Hull seedcrusher living at the newly constructed Swanland House.

In addition Thomas undertook work for the Parish. In 1862 he had twenty two clients on his books.

We have a copy of a bill presented to Thomas by his ironmongers in 1869 (Fig. 24).

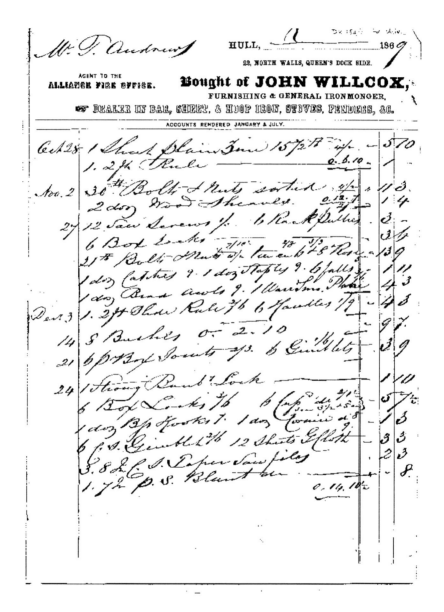

Fig. 24 Thomas Andrew's Ironmonger's Invoice 1869

We also have a random selection of the work he carried out that has been taken from his accounts:

Table 1 Extract from the Accounts of Thomas Andrew.

Date	Client	Work	Cost £ - s - d
02 Jan **1862**	Mr Ringrose	Three new sheep troughs	9 - 8
14 Jan.	G. Westerdale.	Privy door frame.	2 - 6
22 Jan.		To wheels, 4 spokes, felloes	1-12 - 0
17 March	Mr Jackson	Turnip cutter repairs	1 - 0
07 July	Mr Kirby	New trunk locks	1 - 6
08 May	Mr Thompson	New plough beam	6 - 0
31 Jan **1866**	Mr Todd	To carriage	10
17 Aug	Parish	Well repaired	4 - 6

By 1871 Thomas Andrew was also working as a blacksmith, although in a relatively small way. His clients seem to be those he had as a wheelwright. His business included shoeing horses, repairing harrows, and making killing axes, garden scythes and horse traces. He did not appear to remain an ironmonger for long.

The Andrew's business was sited in Main Street, (Fig 34).

Builders and Carpenters

Those responsible for building around Swanland sometimes appear in the Census Returns as Builders, sometimes as Master Bricklayers, suggesting that they were primarily responsible for the bricks, mortar and plaster. Staircases, sash frames, doors and shutters, roofs and floorboards appear to have been the province of the village carpenter, who also made basic furniture.

The earliest reference we have to a builder in Swanland is to Samuel Galland. His account books are available for the early part of the century.[51] In the April and May of 1811 he carried out work on what was then the new Chapel, and also for Mr Todd.

An extract from the accounts illustrates the work for John Todd:

Table 2 Extract from the Accounts of Samuel Galland, 1811

	£ -	s -	d.
Chap 1 day, T Broom 1 day	0	6	10
3 hods lime and hair @ 9d	0	2	3
Chap 1 day, W Poril 1 day	0	6	10
Self 1/2 day At Chimney, Self Do.	0	2	6
To 1 st. whiting @ 1/-	0	1	0
A chimney pot 3/-, journal for Do. 12/6	0	15	6
To 300 st bricks at 4/- per	0	12	0
One st ? at 5d per	0	5	10
	2	12	9

Samuel must have been a man of some substance since his executors' accounts show that they received £865. 5. 7. on his death. Like many of his time he had more than one means of earning a living. He owned two cottages in Hessle, and at least seven acres of land bordering on Westfield Lane, (See Fig 13). On his death his executors received £3. 5. 0 for wheat, and one directory lists him as a farmer.

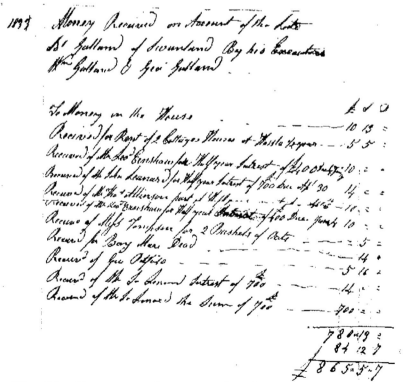

Fig. 25 Executors Accounts for Samuel Galland 1833

From 1841 until the end of the century the builders in the village were the Kirbys. Richard started the business in 1841. His work included the building of the Manor House. [52] By 1881 Richard had been succeeded by his son John.

The carpenters in the village included Habbershaw, whom we have already met as an early wheelwright, but the family, (Samuel and John), were also in the craft. At the end of the century we have the first indication of the Calvert family's involvement.

Fig. 26   John Kirby as a Grand Old Man of 89

Tailors and Dressmakers

Throughout the major part of the nineteenth century the village tailor was George Haldenby. The name prompts the question of whether he was related to the ancient Lords of the Manor, but this appears unlikely as historians tell us that:
.."the [Haldenby] family having flourished.. for many generations, at last for want of a male heir became extinct."[53]

From about 1890 Joseph Marris Frow began to work as a tailor in the village.[54] He lived in the cottage on the corner of West End and Kemp Road, next to the present Post Office. In addition to his business as a tailor, he was sub-postmaster although we are told his wife, in fact, undertook that part of the business. Descendants of the family reside in the village today.

We should mention here the dressmakers and seamstresses, who were notoriously poorly paid. There were at times as many as seven ladies in the village who were thus employed.

Shoemakers

The shoemakers in the latter part of the century included William Newcombe and Robert Wise. William Newcombe ran the first Post Office (Fig. 34).

Undertakers

Death came earlier in the nineteenth century than it does to-day. Samuel Galland recorded the demise of certain of those living in and around the village in his account book, and these are listed at Appendix 5. Accidental deaths included:
"drounded in sistron, kiled [by] Sam Shaws wagon, and died burnt", [his spelling]. Although the village was healthier than the towns, disease was more prevalent than today. In 1878 there was an outbreak of diphtheria in Anlaby, Willerby, and Swanland.[55] Samuel Galland's list affords some idea of life expectancy.

His own funeral came in 1833, and his executors recorded the expenses. They totalled £26.19.10, perhaps £2,000 in to-day's terms, which included for wine, rum, gin, ale, groceries and a butchers bill; a generous wake. Two women and eight bearers attended the funeral, and the expenses also covered these, a coffin, a vault, and "gloves etc." The last item was the most expensive on the list!

The Andrew family whom we have met as wheelwrights, also acted as undertakers. Their records provide a picture of a funeral later in the period. Hannah Billaney wife of Henry Billaney, bailiff at Easenby Farm, died in July 1890, aged only 49. Her funeral included a bill for two pounds of finger biscuits, a bottle of rum, six pocket black border handkerchiefs, and two pairs of cotton gloves, (one youth's). The bearers, who were paid half a crown each, were Messrs Wyse, Beilby, Jewitt, and Crowther.

Shopkeepers

> *"We sell Flour, Barley meal, Pollard, Bran*
> *Bacon, white pease, Cheese, Herrings,*
> *Bread ,Butter, etc.....We keep capital Tea,*
> *Sugar, Tobacco & c....................... .."*

Diary of Robert Sharp, 4th Feb. 1829.

As we have seen, nineteenth century Swanland was a largely self-sufficient community, and included its own shops. In the early part of the century the proprietors were listed as "shopkeepers", and their businesses were perhaps akin to Robert Sharp's in South Cave. They include a James Kemp in 1823.

From mid-century onwards, butchers appear on the Census Returns, one of whom was George Westerdale, who had earlier been in business as a grocer.[56] The siting of George Atkinson's butcher's shop at the end of the century was at the corner of what is now Mere Way, and Main Street, (Fig 34).

In 1882 we find the first reference to a beer retailer, a Selina Anderson who is also a grocer. Perhaps the establishment of the business followed the loss of licence for the Public House, (see below).

The shops of the time had the paned windows of the cottages, rather than the sheet glass windows of today. Window glass was made by hand until the introduction of machinery in about 1905. Some were single storey, with an additional level added in the following century.[57]

The Miller

*"..the building was filled morning, noon, and night
by the music of the mill, the wheels and cogs of
which, being of wood, produced notes that might
have borne a remote resemblance to the wooded
tones of the stopped diapason of the organ."*

Thomas Hardy, The Trumpet Major.

The mill provided the flour for the bread, which formed a vital part of the nation's diet. In 1850 there were 30,000 millers in England.[58]

The first of Swanland's millers were the Beilby family. Thomas was the miller from 1797 through to 1834, when he became bankrupt. In the 1840s and 1850s he was followed by George. The Clayton family ran the business from the 1880s.

Public Houses

The first reference we have to a public house in the township of Swanland appears in Robert Sharp's diary, which provides a graphic account of The *Malt Shovel* at Braffords. It was situated close to the Riplingham Toll Bar on the Kirkella to North Cave turnpike,[59] perhaps a strategic siting for passing travellers. In 1829 he writes:

*"..Chimney piece there is none,…in one corner was a shelf on
which was placed that useful article, a tinder Box, and a shoe
brush or two in a recess,…In the other corner was turned upside
down to hinder the dust from entering, a tin can used for airing
the ale..two or three laths nailed to joists displayed a collection
of old tobacco pipes..".*[60]

Robert describes it as: "a real hedge alehouse". A Robert Stobbart had been innkeeper in Sharp's time, and a John Quest in 1841. The 1881 Census states that Thomas Andrew, the wheelwright, was born there.

Although the *Malt Shovel* continued to be mentioned in the records until the 1890s, after 1841 the occupants are not listed as publicans but as agricultural labourers. Perhaps with the coming of the Hull to Selby Railway in 1840, traffic on the turnpike, and with it trade for the inn, had declined.

Fig. 27 Maud Robinson's Grocery c1913
formerly the White Horse Public House

Swanland's other public house was situated in the centre of the village. From 1841 to 1855 it appears in the records as *The Fleece,* with Gabriel Drew as publican. In 1858 its name changed to *The White Horse,* and John Featherstone, William Hanson and Robert Newby appear in turn as landlords until 1879, after which there is no further reference to it in the Census Returns.

The chief claim to fame of *The White Horse* was the loss of its licence. The reason is given in a cutting believed to come from The Hull News, which states that:

> "..George Filby, Landlord of the White Horse Inn, Swanland was summoned for having on Christmas day…in about one hour's time, supplied a farm labourer Wright, with five or six glasses of whisky …[Wright] afterwards being removed to a stable where he died about three hours subsequently."

Filby was fined, and the following year his licence was rescinded.

The year in which this occurred is uncertain. The cutting from which it is taken has the date 1898 written on it in manuscript, but there is evidence to suggest that it happened earlier. There is no reference to the inn in the Census Return of 1881, and the names of the magistrate who heard the case, the farmer who employed Wright, and shopkeepers who advertised in the newspaper cutting, all appear round about 1879. Shortly afterward Selina Anderson appears as a beer retailer the village.

THE SQUIRES, MINISTERS OF RELIGION & SCHOOLMASTERS

The lives of some villagers are better documented than others because of the position they held in the community. These include the occupants of the Hall and the Manor House, the Ministers of the Independent Chapel, and the village schoolmasters. Any picture of Swanland in the nineteenth century would be incomplete without our meeting them.

The Squires

The Todds - Farmers, Land Proprietors and Barristers

> *"The Todd family did as much for Swanland in the nineteenth century, as the Reckitts were to do in the first thirty years of the twentieth century."*
>
> *John & Christine Wheeler*

One of the oldest families remaining in Swanland in the nineteenth century was that of the Todds. The family could trace their ancestry back to 1625. [61] The earliest record we presently have of them relates to the birth of Thomas Todd in 1706, and appears on the memorial inscription to Thomas and Elizabeth in North Ferriby churchyard.

In the previous century there had been a number of branches of the Todd family living in the village. These included John and Jane, and William and Margaret, as well as Thomas and Elizabeth. [62] The Todds had been farmers. In 1748, land which had been purchased of "..Thomas Todd and William Todd of Swanland" had been sold by Andrew Porrot, of Hull, to establish the Kiplingcotes Plate. This was a horse race to be run each year at Kiplingcotes, and which is still run to this day.

It is with the family of Thomas and Elizabeth that we are concerned for it is their branch of the family that in 1830 purchased Swanland Hall, which was at that time in the hands of the trustees of Nicholas Sykes, a Hull merchant. [63] For most of the nineteenth century their family were the principal residents in the village, and major patrons of the Chapel.

The taxes paid by the Todd family are recorded in the Land Tax Returns of 1773, 1791, 1797, and 1840. [64] Their holdings were extensive and included parts of North Ferriby and the eastern parts of Dairy Cotes. In 1797, it is Mrs Jane Todd, widow of Robert Todd, who is recorded as paying the highest Land Taxes in the village. In 1840, it is she who is listed as owner of Swanland Hall, and her son John, as occupier. In 1823 John was being described as a farmer, but by 1834, he is listed as a member of the "Gentry". At the enclosures of 1837 at least 400 acres are recorded as being awarded to John Todd, establishing good parcels of land to the south and east of the village in exchange for scattered holdings elsewhere. [65] In 1848 he paid property tax on house and buildings of £100, on a farm and two buildings of £30, and a further tax on tenements which were home to nine villagers.

Part of the family tree for Thomas and Elizabeth during the period under review is given in Fig 28 below.

When John Todd senior died in 1871, his son, also named John, inherited the estate. He was a barrister,[66] and had married an Elizabeth Wingfield. They had a daughter, Maria, and a son, John Wingfield Todd. John married again. His second wife was Jane Carlill.

The establishment at the Hall was large. In addition to John Todd senior, the 1851 Census recorded the presence of his son John, his sister, his niece, his granddaughter, two visitors, and four servants. In 1891, in addition to those living at the Hall itself, there were eleven residents at the associated Humberdale farm. These included the foremen, his wife, their five children, a shepherd, and a farm servant.

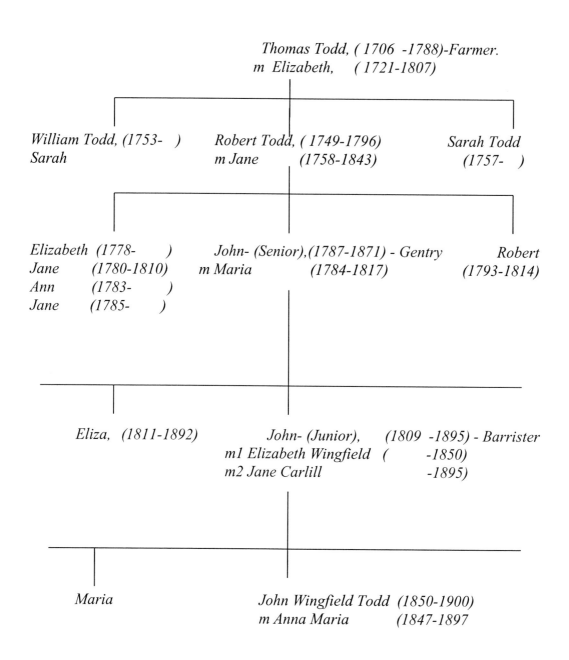

Thomas Todd, (1706 -1788)-Farmer.
m Elizabeth,   (1721-1807)

William Todd, (1753-)   Robert Todd, (1749-1796)   Sarah Todd
Sarah   m Jane   (1758-1843)   (1757-)

Elizabeth (1778-   )   John- (Senior),(1787-1871) - Gentry   Robert
Jane   (1780-1810)   m Maria   (1784-1817)   (1793-1814)
Ann   (1783-   )
Jane   (1785-   )

Eliza,   (1811-1892)   John- (Junior),   (1809 -1895) - Barrister
                               m1 Elizabeth Wingfield   (-1850)
                               m2 Jane Carlill   -1895)

Maria   John Wingfield Todd (1850-1900)
                               m Anna Maria   (1847-1897

Fig. 28   The Todds - Part of their Family Tree

Fig. 29   A Todd Family Group

Members of the Todd family were strongly supportive of the Independent Chapel, in Swanland. From its early days the Todds had been trustees of the chapel, the first mention being of Thomas Todd, on the deed of 1740[67]: his name also appears on that for 1781 together with that of John Todd. The 1821 deed includes John Todd, Gent, Swanland, William Todd, Gent, Turmer Hall, Holderness, John Todd, Tranby Park, Hessle, and William Goodlad Todd, Merchant, Hull. Whitehead,[67] and Patton,[68] make regular references to their gifts in the nineteenth century. Indeed Whitehead considered the chapel to be under the control of the extended Todd family as John Todd of Swanland Hall insisted on paying all chapel expenses, ordinary and special, over and above that raised by the congregation, without special appeal. This was discouraged. Following the death of Eliza Todd, his sister, in 1892, a deed under her will secured several endowments to the chapel, and school. The Rev. Whitehead wrote: "By Miss Eliza Todd's death the chapel and Minister lost their best friend and helper. Her memory will be engraved upon the hearts of all who knew her". As a memorial offering, her brother John put the chapel buildings into thorough repair. Much of the woodwork of the roof and window frames was replaced, and a new heating system supplied. The total cost was £300, this being the last gift by the Todd family to the Independent Chapel.

John Todd and his sister were also loyal supporters and managers of the village school which the Independent Chapel had started in 1694. Throughout the 19th century they made handsome subscriptions towards the cost of running the school. In 1875, after the school had become one inspected by the Government, it was acknowledged that overcrowding was extreme in the existing schoolroom attached to the chapel.[69] John Todd responded to the need for more space by giving some land and paying for a new school building.[70] This is the one by the pond which was formally opened on 3 August 1876, accompanied by a public tea and entertainment paid for by John Todd. The next day the young people had a treat and a ride to Welton Dale in wagons, a tea feast followed by games, distribution of nuts and toys, and the sending forth of splendid balloons in the shapes of elephants, donkeys etc.[71] Initially there was one classroom in the school, but in 1894, following an inspection report of 1892, John Todd paid for an extension to be built to house the infants. His sister on occasions "handed over money [to the managers] to balance the books".[72] as essential expenditure always exceeded income.

Other branches of the family acted as benefactors to the village. A further John Todd, cousin of the Todds at the Hall, lived at Tranby Park, and it was he who in 1827 erected a memorial to the Rev. David Williams, Minister of the Independent Chapel. He also paid for the porches to the Chapel in 1840, and settled £2,000 in trust for the Minister in 1852. The latter had accrued from investment of the legacy in David William's will. Other members of the family lived at Turmer Hall in West Sculcoates, and at Bridlington Quay. The Goodlad Todds have a most impressive family grave in Ferriby churchyard. [73]

Fig. 30 The Todd Family Grave, Ferriby

John Todd died in March 1895, his wife Jane having died in January. Probate was granted in the same year and his effects were estimated at £128,973. 15. 3.[74] Tributes were paid to him by both chapel and school.

The Rev. Whitehead wrote: "Todds' deaths, Mrs Todd Jan.1895, Mr Todd March 1895, and Eliza Todd 1892, were everywhere keenly deplored - the village and chapel suffering great loss. The record herein show that the Todd family had been connected with the chapel from the earliest times".[75]

The school managers wrote: "the school building will remain a monumental witness to the deep interest he, [John Todd], ever took in the welfare of the village."[69]

Although his son, John Wingfield Todd, then took up residence in Swanland Hall and started to participate in village life - he was school manager and founder member of the Parish Council - he lived only until 1900. A later John Wingfield Todd appears not to have had the same interests and the influence of the Todd family on the village of Swanland effectively ceased at the start of the 20th century. The Reckitt family at Swanland Manor assumed their position as philanthropic owners of the principal house in the village. The Todd family finally sold the Hall in 1926.

Sir James Reckitt, 1833 to 1924

Quaker Industrialist and Philanthropist

"Providence has blessed me in a way
Which it has not blessed many others,
And I should be failing in my duty if
I had not done that which I have done."
Sir James Reckitt

James Reckitt came to Swanland in the summer of 1884, purchasing the Manor House from John Davenport. The name of the house changed from that time, becoming known as Swanland Manor. He and his wife Kathleen had four children, Harold, Mary, Philip and Elizabeth.

Born in Nottingham, James was the youngest surviving child of Isaac and Ann Reckitt, a Quaker family whose roots went back to the founding of the movement, (ca 1652). [76] The Quaker background explains much regarding his generous character and that of the family business which his father had founded in Hull.

In 1867, along with his brothers, James inherited the business. He was only 34. The firm which was concerned with the manufacture of starch, laundry blue, and black lead, grew dramatically during the last quarter of the century [77] and its prosperity enabled James to become a major philanthropist. Along with his employees and the people of Hull, the villagers of Swanland were to benefit greatly from his generosity. Much of this fell in the first quarter of the following century, but James had a particular interest in libraries and as early as 1889 a public library was built at his own expense in Holderness Road, Hull. [78]

Within the village we are told that:

> "..every Christmas there was a huge distribution of
> Christmas boxes to those who required help,…one
> Christmas , Sir James varied the usual gifts by presenting
> a library as 'food for the mind', as he had so long comforted
> their bodies with blankets, hams, bread and money. The
> change was sullenly received, for as one villager put it :
> ' ye can't aate beaks. We don't want 'em'."[79]

Fig. 31 James Reckitt about 1885.

Early in the following century Sir James established the Garden Village in East Hull. In February 1907, he wrote to T.R Ferens: "While I and my family are living in beautiful houses surrounded by lovely gardens and fine scenery, the workpeople we employ are, many of them, living in squalor, and all of them without gardens in narrow streets and alleys."[80] In 1914 he provided Swanland with its Village Institute.

James has been described as "…a strong, forceful and even dominating character",[81] and there is evidence to this effect both in the performance of the business and in certain of his letters. Quakers could be disowned for bankruptcy! In 1894, and after some hesitation he accepted a baronetcy, largely for his services to the Liberal Party. In the following year he became the first Chairman of Swanland Parish Council

Although he remained a practising Quaker, he attended the Independent Chapel in the village every Sunday, as well as his own Meeting House in Mason Street, Hull. He was a close friend of the Minister of the Chapel, the Rev. John Whitehead, and the Chapel found James: "…its most generous benefactor. A Church that had every shade of free churchman among its ranks, as well as Anglicans, ..appealed to the broad minded Quaker."[82]

James' funeral in 1924, was held at the Ebenezer Methodist Chapel in Spring Bank, and he was buried in the Quaker Burial Ground nearby. "Vast crowds lined the way to the grave."[83]

Ministers of Religion

Nine Ministers served the Independent Chapel during the years of the nineteenth century. Two of these, the Rev David Williams and the Rev John Whitehead, between them ministered for sixty six years, and because of their long service are best remembered.

The Rev David Williams (Pastorate 1786-1827)

> *"He was descended from an ancient family*
> *in Wales....His character was eminent for*
> *meekness and Catholicity of Spirit, piety,*
> *humility and resignation to the Divine Will;*
> *for thirty nine years he was the faithful Minister*
> *of this village."*

Thus reads the tablet erected in the Independent Chapel in 1827, by John Todd of Tranby Park to the memory of the Rev. David Williams.

David Williams began work at the Chapel in 1786 and together with Thomas Blossom, is reputed in his early years to have established the first Sunday School in the East Riding, [84] (See 18th Century). In 1803 he oversaw the building of the new chapel. [85]

Sadly during his time in the village he was…"called to mourn the death of his wife and all his children: five died at mature ages and one, his only grandchild, in their minority."

The Rev. J. E. Whitehead, (Pastorate 1872 - 1899)
.

The Rev. John Whitehead was the first author of the history of Swanland's Independent Chapel. His manuscript account records: "…not a single line had been written by any of his predecessors.."[86] He was obviously a dedicated historian, as witnessed by his efforts to uncover primary sources of information. The account he left indicates some of the frustration he felt in attempting to re-establish traditional Congregational management to the Chapel.

The Rev. Whitehead played a prominent role in the Board of Management of the School and witnessed the arrival of Government inspection in that establishment, and the building of the new school in 1876.

Schoolmasters

As we have seen earlier the village school in Swanland was established at the same time as the Independent Chapel. There is no clear indication of who the schoolmaster was at the beginning of the nineteenth century, but it may still have been Peter Hodsman who is thought to be Thomas Blossom's teacher. [87] By 1840 a William Cherry appears in the Directories as *schoolmaster*, but as Patton states "…the greatest of the names was that of Richard Witty."

Richard Witty (Schoolmaster 1842-1883)

> *"So [the Chapel] had a Clerk as well as a Minister*
> *… whose business it was to strike the time..sometimes*
> *with a fiddle, and to make announcements,*
> *occasionally banns of marriage, and keep minutes..*
> *To these duties, later was appended the role of*
> *Schoolmaster. The greatest of such names was Richard*
> *Witty."*
>
> *A Country Independent Chapel - Rev, J Patton.*

Richard Witty was born in 1810,[88] and appointed village schoolmaster in about 1842. In addition to his duties as schoolmaster he was also "Acting" Deacon of the Chapel, local village Registrar, and surveyor of Roads, "in which he exercised much authority". He retired from the position of schoolmaster at the age of 73.

He has been described as "…a man of trusted integrity, whose old world dignity and authority were thoroughly reverenced in the community." George Westerdale, Percy Westerdale, Charley Andrew and Harry Hotham were numbered among his pupils.[89]

He held his position at the school from the time it operated in the original schoolhouse, until after the new school was built by the pond. He found the inspections, after 1871 a great trial and must have found it very hard teaching children of all ages in the one schoolroom.

William Beynon (Schoolmaster 1883 - 1913)

*"Here we suffer grief and pain
Under Billy Beynon's cane."*

Discovered on the inside of a Bible in Christ Church.

William Beynon from Llanelly succeeded Mr Witty. His wife was also appointed Sewing Mistress. Their joint salary in 1883 was £60. To this was added the whole of the school pence money, (money collected from parents), and half the grant received from the government, (in 1892 this was £ 62. 1. 0). Their income was therefore dependent on the results achieved by the pupils. During his time at the school standards improved and satisfactory reports were received from the School Inspectors.

COMMUNICATIONS

An account of the roads in and around Swanland has been given in the earlier chapter describing life in the eighteenth century. They were improved at the time of the enclosure awards.

At the beginning of the nineteenth century the means of travel for ordinary villagers was largely by foot. It was not unusual to walk long distances. Thomas Blossom on leaving Swanland in 1798: "…walked all night and was within four miles of York by seven or eight o'clock on Monday morning."[90] Robert Sharp occasionally travelled from South Cave to Beverley on foot, a distance of nine and a half miles.[91]

For those who did not wish to walk, or where goods were to be moved, there was always the village carrier. People were dependent on the carrier for supplies from the nearest town. In 1892 the carrier in Swanland was William Dowson. He was related by marriage to the Brooks family, whose descendants still reside in the village. The carrier went to Hull on Tuesdays and Fridays, and to Beverley on Saturdays.

The first horse drawn omnibus service to Swanland was provided by Thomas Fillingham in 1831, (Fig 32). His booking office in Hull was in Carr Lane.[92]

Wealthier villagers had their horses or carriages; the farmer his pony and trap. A newspaper article from early in following century describes Mr Brough Watson and his pony:

> "Mr Watson rode an old black pony: he was rarely seen
> on foot except to attend the chapel services, which he did
> regularly….He visited the butcher's shop every Friday
> morning to order his meat and see it weighed. I believe
> the hook is still in the wall where he hung the bridle of his
> pony."[93]

By 1840 it was possible for a villager to walk down the hill to Ferriby, and catch a train to Selby, Leeds, and York "without change of carriage."[94] The presence of a railway so close to the village was used to advantage by the estate agents of the day, whose bills of sale made reference to the fact. When Northfield House was sold in 1869, it was advertised as: "…being situate in the immediate neighbourhood of the Mansions and Parks of the resident gentry, and within easy reach of the railway station of Ferriby and Hessle."

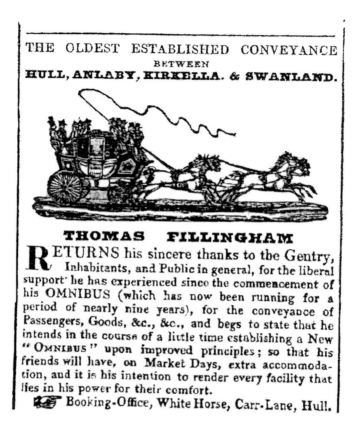

Fig. 32 Thomas Fillingham's Omnibus

By 1841, at certain times of the tide, five or six steam packets could be seen: "..urging their way up and down [the river], in the course of an hour. During the same time, probably three trains would pass you upon the railroad..the latter remarkably contrasting its rapidity of transit with the former."[95]

THE VILLAGE AT THE END OF THE CENTURY

"The period was a very ferment of change.
The epithet 'new' was applied to the age and
to almost everything to do with it. Politics,
the Unions, women, art, fiction, paganism,
Hedonism, realism, drama, the very spirit of
the times were all new."

Holbrook Jackson. The Eighteen Nineties.

The 1890s were the period in which a new political party arose, Art Nouveau flourished, and Oscar Wilde's aestheticism captured London. So far as is known, such events did not interfere with the quiet tenor of life in Swanland.

There were some changes. The most important of these was perhaps the creation of the Parish Council, although it had limited powers. Parish Councils were established through the Local Government Act of 1894, and the first meeting in Swanland was on the 4 January 1895. Sir James Reckitt was elected chairman, and William Beynon the village schoolmaster, acted as clerk. The business of the Council largely falls into the succeeding chapter, but in its early days a major concern was a piped water supply.[67] A new water tower for the village had been built in West End, in 1884.

In the 1890's, the grand houses with their estates were intact. Sir James Reckitt of Reckitt's Blue and Reckitt's Starch is still at Swanland Manor, and has acquired much of the land and property to the west of the village. Andrew Duncan, the seed crusher is at Swanland House. John Todd , barrister and magistrate is at the Hall, and John Shaw, a corn merchant at the former Northfield House, now called Beech Hill.

It is possible to form a picture of the village at this time by superimposing the names of villagers from the 1891 Census on the Ordnance Survey Map of 1888,
(Fig 34). There is now a Post Office in Swanland, although postal orders and telegrams have to be handled by North Ferriby. Ironically for *The Naughty Nineties*, the public house has been lost, but Selina Anderson, grocer, supplies the village's needs for beer. The new model farms appear.

Village craftsmen still flourish. Henry Beilby is the blacksmith, William Andrew the wheelwright and Robert Wise the shoemaker.

The age of the motor car is not yet with us, and there is no tarmac on the roads William Mayhew is coachman at Swanland Manor, and Joseph Dennett at The Hall.

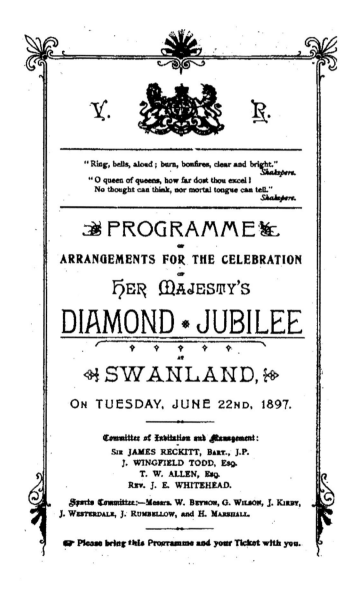

Fig. 33   Diamond Jubilee Celebrations, 1897

Public services are minimal, and although six standpipes had been provided at the time the water tower was built, the village still relies on its wells and cisterns. The Manor has its own gasworks and William Farmery works as a gasmaker in the village. The Manor House and Hall are the first to benefit from dynamos, powered by oil engines. It is claimed that the Manor House was one of the first in the county to have this provision.[68] Mr W.H Calvert lays the wiring.

In 1897 the village, along with the rest of the nation, celebrated the Queen's Diamond Jubilee, with many of our old friends mentioned in the programme. It perhaps provides a fitting finale to our visit to a hundred years of the villages history.

It is thus we leave the nineteenth century. In the coming quarter century the world is to change, and with it a way of life. Mains sewerage, electricity and the motor car are soon to appear in the village, and within forty years it is to more than double its population.

"'Tis well an old age is out, time to begin anew."

References for the Nineteenth Century

1. Baines, *Yorkshire, Vol.2, E & N Ridings*, 1823, p394

2. Rev D J Bulman, *North Ferriby: A Villagers History*,
    Lockington Publishing Co. 1982, p22

3. K J Allison, *Hull Gent Seeks Country Residence, 1750-1850*
    Beverley, East Yorkshire Local History Society 1981,p42

4. D.O.E. *Site and Monuments Record 5794*,
    Humberside County Architects Department, 1988

5. *Land Tax Assessment for Swanland 1797*,
    Hull City Archives, DMX268/46

6. Thomas Jeffreys, *The County of York Surveyed, 1775*
    Hull, Local Studies Library.

7. The Hull Advertiser, 14:1:1825 and 8:7:1825

8. Baines, op.cit.

9. *Census for 1841*, Swanland

10. *Census for 1871*, Swanland

11. Janice & Peter Crowther, *The Diary of Robert Sharp of South Cave*,
    Oxford, Oxford University Press, 1997, p43

12. *Ferriby and Swanland, Kirkella & Westella Enclosure Award 1837*,
    East Riding of Yorkshire Archives, Beverley, PE 36/38.

13. *Bacon to Watson, Conveyance*,
    East Riding of Yorkshire Archives, Beverley, DDMT/229.

14. S Mason, *Social and Economic History*,
    Basingstoke, Macmillan Press Ltd, 1988, p35.

15. Thomas Blossom, op.cit.p236

16. *Map of Ancient Enclosure in the Township of Swanland subject to Tithe, 1840*.
    Borthwick Institute, York.

17. *East Riding Registry of Deeds*,
    Vol FK, P365, No 412

18. *Enclosure Award 1837*, op.cit. p260

19.   *Whites Directory, 1840,*
       Wauldby

20.   *Hull Daily News Supplement*, 12th October, 1895.

21.   D Chapman- Huston, *Sir James Reckitt - A Memoir*,
      London, Faber & Gwyer, 1924, p203.

22.   ibid, p203

23.   *Hull Times*, 5th April 1924, p203

24.   ibid

25.   E Walford M.A. *The County Families 1881*

26.   J G Hall, *The History of South Cave*,
      Hull, Edwin Ombler, 1892, p240

27.   *Hull Times*, 5th April 1924

28.   idem

29.   J G Hall, op.cit. p241

30.   *Plan of an Estate at Swanland belonging to Miss Thomson, 1861*,
      Hull City Archives, DBHT 12/12/25

31.   *Census for 1841*, Swanland

32.   K J Allison, op.cit. p42

33.   John Henry Whiting, *Portraits of Public Men*, p10
      Hull, Free Press Office, 1858, p10

34.   Hull City Archives, DBHT/9/116

35.   J G Patton, *A Country Independent Chapel*,
      A Brown & Sons 1943, pp28-9.

36.   J E Whitehead, *Records of the Congregational Church assembling at Swanland
      In the East Riding of Yorkshire, 1899.*
      (Manuscript at Christ Church).

37.   J E Whitehead, ibid

38.   J G Patton, op.cit. p29

39.   John Richardson, *The Local Historians Encyclopaedia*,
      London, Historical Publications Ltd. 1999, p225

40.   *Land Tax Assessment for Swanland 1797, op.cit.*

41. *Hull Daily Mail*, 22 nd December, 1948.

42. *Bill of Sale for Swanland Mill, 1860,*
    Copy located at Skidby Mill, also in Hull Advertiser.

43 *The Miller*, 4th January 1909.

44. Janice and Peter Crowther, op.cit. pxxxvi

45. Janice and Peter Crowther, ibid, p86

46. Geoffrey Best, *Mid Victorian Britain, 1851-75,*
    London, Fontana Press,1979, p116

47. Thomas Blossom, *The Life of Mr T Blossom* (a transcript dated 1895 of
    Mr Blossom's autobiographical manuscript) in Local Notes Vol:2 by
    W Richardson, a hand written compilation,
    Hull Central Library, p113-115.

48. David Souden, *The Victorian Village,*
    Brockhampton Press, 1995, p96.

49. Roger Mason, *Granny's Village,*
    London, Macdonal Futura, 1980, pp 55-60

50. *Papers of the Andrew Family of Swanland ,*
    University of Hull Archives, DX/184

51. *The Executors' Accounts for Samuel Galland of Swanland,*
    Kingston upon Hull Local Studies Library, L4659, L920 GAL.P

52. *Hull Times*, 5th April, 1924.

53. George Hadley, *A New and Complete History ...of the Town of Kingston upon Hull,*
    Lowgate, T.Briggs, 1788, p849.

54.   Bulmer, *Swanland History, Topography and Directory of East Yorkshire (with Hull),*
    1892.

55. Outbreak *of Diphtheria, Anlaby, Willerby, Swanland,*
    Hull Times, 27thJuly, 1878.

56.   Census for 1841, Swanland.

57. J G Patton, op.cit. facing p11.

58. David Souden, op.cit. p102.

59. *The Malt Shovel*, Ordnance Survey Map 1855.

60. Janice & Peter Crowther, op.cit. p192

61. J G Patton, op.cit. p20

62. *The Baptismal Register*, Christ Church, Swanland.

63. K J Allison, op.cit. p42.

64. *Land Tax Assessment for Swanland* , DMX 268/10, DMX 268/29, DMX 268/46
                                DMX 268/50, DMX268/63
    Hull City Archives.

65. *Enclosure Award 1837,* op.cit. pp157-58.

66. *Census for 1851*, Swanland.

67. J E Whitehead, op.cit.

68. J G Patton, op.cit.

69. *Swanland School Managers' Minute Book 1871- 1898*, SL 105/107,
    East Riding of Yorkshire Archives Office, Beverley.

70. J E Whitehead, op.cit.

71. *Swanland Parish Council Minutes,*
    East Riding of Yorkshire Archives Office, Beverley.

72. *Swanland School Managers' Minute Book 1889,*
    East Riding of Yorkshire Archives Office, Beverley

73. *North Ferriby Monumental Inscriptions,*
    East Yorkshire Family History Society, p36.

74. *Probate Returns, 1895,*
    East Riding of Yorkshire Archive Office, Beverley.

75. J E Whitehead, op.cit.

76. Dr B N Reckitt, *A History of the Sir James Reckitt Charity, 1921-1979,*
    Hull, White & Farrell Ltd. 19

77. Dr B N Reckitt, *The History of Reckitt & Sons Ltd.,*
    London, A.Brown and Son Ltd. 1965, p47.

78. *Ours*, The House Magazine of Reckitt & Sons, September 1934, p125.

79. J G Patton, op.cit. p61

80. Dr B N Reckitt, *The History of Reckitt & Sons Ltd.,*op.cit., p60.

81. Dr B N Reckitt, *A History of the Sir James Reckitt Charity, 1921-1979*, op.cit.p6

82. J G Patton, op.cit. p59.

83. J G Patton, ibid, p62.

84. J E Whitehead, op.cit.

85. J E Whitehead, ibid, p5.

86. J E Whitehead, ibid, p1

87. J G Patton, ibid, p63

88. J G Patton, ibid, p55.

89. J G Patton, ibid, p64.

90. Thomas Blossom, op.cit. p125

91. Janice & Peter Crowther, op.cit.

92. *Hull Advertiser*, 3rd January 1840.

93. *Hull Times* , 5th April 1924.

94. Rev D Bulman, op.cit. p81

95. *The Strangers Guide to Ferriby, Welton, Elloughton and South Cave*,
     Sold by J Bayner, Hull etc. 1841.

APPENDIX 1: WINDOW TAX RECORDS FOR SWANLAND

Hull Archives Reference CT 102-140

WINDOW TAX 1774

Swanland Windows and Lights for ye Year of Our Lord 1774

Assessors and collectors are: John Turner   Abraham X Dixon
(his ... mark)

		Windows	£	s	d
John Beecroft		6	0	3	0
John Atkinson	*Power**	0	0	0	0
Timothy Moment	*Power*	0	0	0	0
Hannah Shaw	*Power*	0	0	0	0
John Bayler	*Power*	0	0	0	0
Mr Tuff		11	0	14	0
Mr Broadley House		7	0	4	2
John Watson		15	1	5	6
John Todd		7	0	4	2
John Kelsey	*Power*	0	0	0	0
John Hodsman	*Power*	0	0	0	0
John Wood	*Power*	0	0	0	0
Wm. Galland		9	0	9	0
George Berridge		11	0	14	0
Abraham Dixon		7	0	4	2
James Kemp		7	0	4	2
John Westerdale		7	0	4	2
Elizabeth Plaister	*Power*	0	0	0	0
Tho. Dixon		5	0	3	0
Ms Hall		7	0	4	2
Samuel Watson		11	0	14	0
Thos Bibbings		7	0	4	2
Thos Turner		7	0	4	2
Thos Featherstone		6	0	3	0
John Todd Snr		7	0	4	2
John Briggs		6	0	3	0
Mr Geo Hall		15	1	5	6

*Power = Poor

		Windows	£	s	d
Thos Shaw		11	0	14	0
Thos Galland		8	0	9	0
John Martin	*Power*	0	0	0	0
W Watson		9	0	9	0
Henry Stappelton		6	0	3	0
John Bellard		6	0	3	0
Wm. Bullock		7	0	4	2
Richard Hardy		6	0	3	0
Thos Todd		15	1	5	6
John Draper	*Power*	0	0	0	0
Thos Beecroft		6	0	3	0
Wm. Shaw		5	0	3	0
Wm. Todd		11	0	14	0
Mr John Porter Esq.		41	4	5	0
Andrew Bilton		5	0	3	0
David Freeman		7	0	4	2
Frances Thomson		6	0	3	0
Peter Handerson		4	0	3	0
Thomas Wilberforce	*Power*	0	0	0	0
John Featherstone		4	0	3	0
Newington John Hornby		10	0	11	4
Tho Rosendal		7	0	4	0
			† £17	16	10

† This total should be £17.18.10

WINDOW TAX 1779

Swanland

		Windows	£	s	d
John Beecroft		6	0	3	0
Robert Chidson	Poor	-	-	-	-
Robert Sedgwhick	Poor	-	-	-	-
Minister House	Empty	-	-	-	-
William Watson	Poor	-	-	-	-
John Watson		15	1	5	6
John Todd		8	0	7	0
Robert Serginson	Poor	-	-	-	-
John Bellard		6	0	3	0
William Galland		7	0	4	2
Thomas Watson		14	1	4	0
Abraham Dixon		7	0	4	2
John Westerdale		7	0	4	2
James Kemp		7	0	4	2
John Bullock		5	0	3	0
Samuel Watson		11	0	14	0
Nathaniel Willson		6	0	3	0
Thos Turner		7	0	4	2
Thos Featherstone	Poor	-	-	-	-
John Hodsman		5	0	3	0
Thos Todd		6	0	3	0
John Briggs		6	0	3	0
Mr Geo Hall		16	1	7	0
Thomas Shaw		11	0	14	0
Thos Galland		8	0	7	0
William Watson		9	0	9	0
Henry Stapelton		6	0	3	0
Richardson Stephenson		8	0	7	0
George Berridge		6	0	3	0
Richard Hardy	Poor	-	-	-	-
Robert Todd		15	1	5	6
John Draper	Poor	-	-	-	-
Thomas Beecroft		6	0	3	0
William Shaw		5	0	3	0
			10	13	10

	Windows	£	s	d
William Todd	11	0	14	0
Robert Clark	5	0	3	0
John Porter Esq.	41	4	5	0
David Freeman	7	0	4	2
Francis Thomson *Poor*	-	-	-	-
Peter Anderson	4	0	3	0
Thomas Wilberfors *Poor*	-	-	-	-
Newington	10	0	11	4
Thomas Rosingdale	7	0	4	2
		£16	18	6

Swanland Assessors for Windows and Lights
for the year 1779 are: John Turner

his
Abrm. x Dixon
mark

APPENDIX 2: LAND TAX ASSESSMENTS

FOR THE TOWNSHIP OF

SWANLAND

FOR THE YEARS 1791 AND 1797

Land Tax Assessment for the Township of Swanland in the County of the Town of Kingston upon Hull after the rate of four Shillings for Pound for the Year 1791

	£ s	£ s d
John Todd for J. Adams Boynton Esqr Farm	18 10	3 16
Do for East part of East Dary gate	11	2 4
Do for R C Broadley Esqr Farm	9 14	2 7 8
Do for upper Jockley	8	1 12
John Watson for his Farm	19 10	3 18
Samℓ Watson for his Farm	18 18½	3 15 8
Do for Dixon Land	7½	1 6
Do for South Jockley	5	1
Do for 17th of Meadow in 10 Ings	2	8
Do for J Adams Boynton Esqr Wood	1 15	7
John Turner for part of Norrisons Farm	7 10	1 10
Do for J Sykes Esqr part of Pease Farm	6	1 4
Do for a House	15	3
Do for J R Pease Esqr Land	10	2
Do for J Turner Land	15	3
John Ringrose for his Farm & Tythe	45	9
Do for Pickering Farm	9 10	1 18
Do for Sir H E Thorington part of Pease	1	6
Wm Ha sen for J Sykes Esqr Watton Farm	16 5	3 5
Do for Stapleton Land	15	3
Robℓ Load for Tythe	33 16½	6 15 4
Do for Farm Jub Wood & Dams Farm	43 13½	8 14 8
Do for Eckroft & Meadow	1	4
Thoℓ Shaw for Sillingston Farm	43 15	8 15
Do for his own Farm	12 13½	2 10 8
Do for part of Breerch 4 Land	5 13½	1 2 8
Do for Tythe of Humber Closes	1	4
Mrs Call for Bibbings House & Land	1 15	7
Do for Stapleton House	1 5	5
Carrd forwd		

Description	£	s	£	s	d
Bro[ought] forwd					
John Porter Esqr for his Hall & Ground	7	10	1	10	
Do for part of Pease Farm	2	10		10	
Do for part of Norrison Farm	10	10	2	2	
Do for Bullock Farm	7			18	
Do for Nicholson Close	2	10		10	
Do for Broad Ley Close	1	5		5	
Do for Fowler Close	1			4	
Thos Brigham for a House		15		3	
John Blossom for a House		10		2	
Staph Atkinson for a House		10		2	
Wm Galland for House & Land	3			12	
Jo Hemp for Land		10		2	
John Westerdale for his Houses & Land	3			12	
Do for Brickcliff Land	1	10		6	4
John Bullock for a House		15		3	
Thos Beelby for House & Land	1	15		7	
Robt Galland for Land	4	5		17	
Thos Beecroft for House & Land	1	5		5	
Mr Shaw for House & Land	1	5		5	
Wm Walker for Land	5		1		
Mrs Allenson for Close & Meadow	3			12	
Jas Sykes Esqr for Tythe in W Ings	4			16	
Do for Galland Houses & Close	1	15		7	
Wm Glaiton for Land		5		1	
Jno Leslett for Land	1	10		4	4
Wm Green for Mans Dale	1	15		7	
Do for Land	1	10		7	
Anthony Brough for Land		15		3	
John Spicer for Land		8	4	1	8
John Carlill for Land		5		1	
Robt Brough for Fairycoats & Maker	12	10	2	10	4
Do for Land	1	15		7	
John Robinson for Land		17	6	3	6
Thos Robinson for Hall of Mans Dale		17	6	3	6
Jos Robinson Pease Esqr for Land	4			16	
Wm Bilton for Brocklebank Land		8	4	1	8
Mr Coultas for Meadow in W Ings		5		1	
Carrd forwd					

Description	£	s		d
Bro forwd				
Occupr of Wm Stocks Meadow in W Ings	1	~	~	4
Occupr of Wm Stockdale Meadow in Ings	2	~	~	8
Occuprs of Wm Ings	13	10	2	14
Occupr of Wm Brassfords	13	~	2	12
Occupr of Oxengates	3	~	~	12
Do of Gurnby Land	1	5	~	5
Do of 2 Rooth of Meadow in W Ings	~	10	~	2
John Infield for Dairy coats & 20 of Mead	14	~	2	16
Occupr of Trinity House Land	3	~	~	12
Richd Wilson for hill Flatt	1	10	~	6
Henry Watson for part of Pearse Farm	4	10	~	18
Do for Nicholson part of Sam Farm	3	2½	~	12	6
Do for Land	~	10	~	2
Do for Nicholson Meadow	~	8¾	~	1	8
Francis Crathorn for Land	~	10	~	2
Sam Harrison for York Grounds	11	~	2	4
Do for East Stockley	6	13¾	1	6	8
Mr Williamson for Welton Grounds	20	~	4	~
Francis Brough for Wreays	14	~	2	16
Do for East Wood Close	2	~	~	8
Mr Cross for Tythe	1	5	~	5
Peter Atkinson for his Farm & Wood	13	~	2	12
Mr Wakefield for Tythe of part Wreays & Tod	2	15	~	11
		£ 110	8	8

Robt Todd
William Watson } Surveyors

Land tax Assessment for the Township of Swanland in the County of the Town of Kingston upon Hull after the rate of four Shillings in the Pound for the year 1797 —

	£	s		£	s	d
Thomas Beilby for his House & Mill	1	—			4	—
Samuel Galland for House & Close	1	—			4	—
Timothy Reeves for his own House	1	5			5	—
Do for R C Broadley Esqr Farm	23	—		4	12	—
Oxgd of Turner Meadow	1	—			4	—
Thos Shaw for H Watson Farm	18	10		3	14	—
Do for part of Pease Farm	4	10			18	—
Do for Nicholson part of Dam Farm	3	2/6			12	6
Do for Nicholson Meadow	—	8/6			1	8
Wm Mitchell for Jocelyn Price Esqr Farm	18	10		3	14	—
Do for York Grounds	12	—		2	8	—
Do for upper Jockley	8	—		2	8	—
Do for South Jockley	3	—			12	—
Do for east Jockley	6	13/4		1	6	8
Do for Wood	1	15			7	—
Do for Tythe of Jockley	—	8/4			1	8
James Kemp for Land	—	10			2	—
John Westerdale for House & Land	3	—			12	—
Do for part of Briercliff Land	1	1/8			6	4
John Bullock for House & Garth	—	15			3	—
Hannah Newlove for Mr S Watson Farm	20	—		4	—	—
Do for Dixon Land	—	7/6			1	6
Do for Father House & Land	3	—			12	—
Thomas Chapman for House & Close	1	—			4	—
John Turner for Mr Sykes Land	2	6/8			9	4
Do for his own Land	—	15			3	—
Do for a House	—	15			3	—
John Briggs for House & Land	1	15			7	—
John Ringrose for Farm & Tythe	45	—		9	—	—
Do for Pickering Farm	9	10		1	18	—
Do for Sir W Etherington part of Pease Farm	1	—			4	—
Mr Marshall for his Father Farm	12	13/4		2	10	8
Do for part of Briercliff Land	5	13/4		1	2	8
Carr Forward £						

	£	s	d		£	s	d	
Bro:t forward								
W:m Watkinson for Jos. Sykes Esq:r Farm	12	5			2	9		
D:o for Massey Close	2	—			—	8		
D:o for Stapleton Land	—	15			—	3		
John Todd for Stapleton House	1	5	—		—	5		
D:o for R Esten Land	—	5			—	1		
D:o for Jn:o Green Land	—	17/6	—		—	3	6	
D:o for Tho:s Scott Land	1	18			—	4	4	
Mr:s Todd for Tythe	33	16/8			6	15	4	
D:o for Farm Ireb Wood & Dam Farm	43	13/4			8	14	8	
D:o for Jos:t Robinson Pease Esq:r Land	—	10			—	2		
D:o for Cockcroft & Meadow	1	—			—	4		
D:o for upper Dale closes	2	—			—	8		
D:o for Whitton Leys	—	15	—		—	3	—	
D:o for Land	—	10			—	2		
Mary Becroft for House & Land	1	5			—	5		
Mr Shaw for House & Land	1	5			—	5		
Thomas Shaw for Lillingston Farm	43	15			8	15		
D:o for Tythe of Holmber Closes	1	—			—	4	—	
Mr:s Porter for House & Ground	7	10			1	10		
D:o for Part of Pease Farm	2	10	—		—	10	—	
D:o for part of Norrison Farm	10	10			2	2		
D:o for Bullock Farm	7	—			1	8	—	
D:o for Nicholson Close	2	10	—		—	10	—	
D:o for Broadley Close	1	5	—		—	5	—	
D:o for Dickinson House	1	—			—	4	—	
D:o for Fowler Close	1	—			—	4	—	
Benj:n Wilson for a Close	3	—	—		—	12	—	
Jos Sykes Esq:r for Tythe in Would Ings	4	—			—	16	—	
D:o for Galland Houses & Close	1	15	—		—	7	—	
W:m Green for Scatchard Meadow	2	—			—	8	—	
W:m Green, Hessle for Land	1	16/8			—	7	4	
D:o for Brocklebank Land	—	8/4	—		—	1	8	
Thomas Robinson for half of Marsh Dale	—	17/6	—		—	3	6	
Robert Brough for Dairy coats & Rakes	12	11/8			2	10	4	
D:o for Land	1	15			—	7		
...Brough for Land	1	5	—		—	5		
Anthony ... for Land	—	5	—		—	1	—	
Jn:o Caskell for Land	2	8/4			—	1	8	
Jn:o Spicer for Land	—	8/4			—	3	16	
Jn:o Kid for Dairy coats & Rakes	14				3	16	—	
Carr:d forward £								

	£	s	d	£	s	d
Bro't forw'd						
R. C. Threadley Esqr for Manfield Dale	1	15	–		7	–
Do for Jetison Meadow	1	10	–		6	–
Do for Coulter Meadow	–	5	–		1	–
Henry Watson for Land	–	10	–		2	–
Stephen Gray for Trinity House Land	3	–	–		12	–
Mr Heppleden for Dairy coats	11	–	2		4	–
Do for 17 Acres of Meadow	2	–	–		8	–
Richard Wilson for Hill Flatt	1	10	–		6	–
Do Mr Hall Land	1	–	–		4	–
Saml G. Watson for Welton Grounds	20	–	–	4	–	
Peter Anderson for his Farm & Wood	13	–	–	2	12	
Francis Brough for Wreays	14	–	–	2	16	
Do for East Wood Close	2	–	–		8	–
Do for Tythe of Wreays	–	13	11	–	2	8
Thos Wilson for Tythe of Brafford	–	13	4	–	2	8
Revd R. Cross for Tythe	1	5	–		5	–
Mr Galland for Land	3	10	–		14	–
J. R. Pease Esqr for Land	4	–	–		16	–
Francis Crathorn for Land	–	10	–		2	–
John Theedam for Newington	13	10	–	2	14	
Occupr of Oxengate &c	3	–	–		12	–
Do of two Rooth of Meadow in Ings	–	10	–		2	–
John Hudson for Strakes Meadow	1	–	–		4	–
Mr Mace for Nt Brafford	13	–	–	2	12	–
				110	8	8

John Turner
Timothy Reeves } Assessors

1797 } Allowed by us

APPENDIX 3

The 'Swanland Rental' of 1779:
Transcript of an original in the East Riding Registry of Deeds,
being a list of inhabitants and the rental value of the property they occupied,
compiled in connection with their liability to maintain local roads.

Swanland Rentle

A list of the rentle on Lands and Inhabitants of the Township and Constabulary of Swanland for the Year of Our Lord 1779:

William Todd		£200
Robert Todd	£320	£400
William Shaw		4
Robert Clerk		-
Thomas Buttle		-
John Draper		-
Henry Stappleton		6
Richard Stephenson		-
George Berridge		-
George Hall		150
John Porter		20
Thomas Shaw	£150	120
Thomas Galland		6
John Briggs		5
John Blossom		-
John Hodsman		-
Thomas Turner		130
Samuel Watson		60
William Watson		5
John Westerdale		-
Abraham Dixon		6
James Hemp		-
John Bullock		-
William Galland		10
Thomas Newlove		-
Thos Watson		20
John Bellard		-
William Burril		-
John Wood		-

`Thos Burril	8	
John Todd	150	
John Watson	130	
Robert Serginson	-	
John Moment	-	
Thos Rosingdale	-	
David Freeman	70	
Peter Anderson	40	
Thomas Wilberforce	-	
Francis Hopper	32	
Occup of York Grounds	28	
John Martin	40	
Joseph Watson	10	
Peter Brough	40	
John Jewitt	45	
Occup of Newington	40	
Samuel Harrison	20	
Mr Wakefield	20	
Thos Featherstone	-	
Henry Watson	-	
Richard Scruton	6	
Matt Johnson	12	
John Robinson	4	
Robert Levitt	6	
William Bilton	3	
John Spicer	2	
Anthony Brough	6	10
William Green	10	10
Thos Dixon	-	
John Crathorn	2	10
Robert Chidson	-	

John Turner, one of the Surveyors of the Highways of Swanland, maketh Oath that the list of the others dede is a true list of all person liable to do Statute work upon the Highways within the township constablerys of Swanland and the Rents that each respective person is liable to perform Statute duty for to the best of his knowledge and belief

John Turner

22 June 1779
before me Isaac Broadley

VILLAGE OCCUPATIONS IN THE NINETEENTH CENTURY

APPENDIX 4

	1841	1851	1861	1871	1881	1891
Farmers or *Bailiffs/ Hind*						
1. Braffords	Atkinson William	Jackson Charles	Jackson Charles	Blythe John	Blythe John	*Mennell William*
2. York Grounds					*Boothby Thomas*	*Boothby Thomas*
3. Swanland Dale	Thompson John	Thompson John	Thompson John	Thompson John	Dunn Daniel	Dunn Daniel
4. Swanland Dale					Lister Foster	Lister Foster
5. Swanland Field					*Briggs Robert*	*Briggs Robert*
6. Humber Field	Clark John	Clark John				
7. Humber Dale			*Featherstone Robert*	*Caley Henry*	*Caley Henry*	*Caley Henry*
8. Northfield House	Shaw Nathaniel	Shaw Nathaniel	Shaw Nathaniel			Marshall Francis
9. Easenby		Wallis John	Wallis John			*Billaney Henry*
10. Not Known	Usher Robert	Usher Elizabeth				
11. Not Known	Westerdale Thomas	Westerdale Thomas				
12. Not Known	Crowther James					
13. Tank Farm	Fillingham Thomas	Fillingham Thomas		Attenborough Richard	Dowson William	
14. Not Known	Chatterton John					
15. Not Known	Shipley Thomas					
16. Not Known	Hardy Henry					
17. Not Known			Ringrose Robert			
18. The Manor Fram			*Jackson Charles*		*Jackson Charles*	*Jackson Charles*
19. Not Known			Robwell Thomas			
20. Not Known			Whitaker Samuel			
21. Not Known			Featherstone Thomas			Featherstone Thomas
22. Not Known			*Peat James*			
23. Not Known					Westerdale John	Westerdale John
24. Not Known						*Andrew William*
25. Mere House?						
26. Not Known					Cartill John	
27. Wauldby Hall					Drewery Thomas	
28. Not Known					Botteril Richard	
29. Swanland Hall					Dunn George	*Dennett Samuel*
30. Westfield [Wold]						Heron Jane
31. Not Known					*Evison John*	
32. Model Manor						*Cowper Edward* [Sir James Reckitt]

APPENDIX 4

VILLAGE OCCUPATIONS IN THE NINETEENTH CENTURY

	1841	1851	1861	1871	1881	1891
Blacksmiths						
1.	Boyes Richard	Blakey William	Blakey William		Beilby Henry	Beilby Henry
2.	Westerdale George	Andrew Thomas	Beilby Henry	Andrew Thomas	Andrew Thomas	Andrew William
3.			Holiday William			
Wheelwrights						
1.		Andrew Thomas	Andrew Thomas	Andrew Thomas	Andrew Thomas	Andrew William
2.			Westerdale Samuel	Andrew William		
3.				Andrew Charles		
Builders						
1.	Richards Francis	Kirby Richard	Newcombe John	Kirby John	Kirby John	Sellars John
2.	Downs George		Harper Mark			Beilby James
3.	Barker John					
Carpenters / Joiners						
1.	Crowther John	Smith Thomas	Beecroft Henry		Westerdale Samuel	Calvert Walter
2.	Grey John	Turner John			Westerdale John	Calvert William
3.	Habbershaw William	Habbershaw William			Walker James	
4.	Turner John	Westerdale Samuel				
5.	Petfield William	Condor Thomas				
6.	Webb John					
Tailors						
1.	Haldenby George	Haldenby George	Haldenby George	Haldenby George	Haldenby George	Haldenby George
2.	Pool Francis	Hance James				
3.	Pool John					Frow Joseph
4.	Wilson Thomas					

VILLAGE OCCUPATIONS IN THE NINETEENTH CENTURY

APPENDIX 4

	1841	1851	1861	1871	1881	1891
Shoemakers						
1.	Speck Thomas	Newcombe William		Newcombe William [Also Post Office]	Newcombe William [Also Post Office]	Newcombe William [Also Post Office]
2.	Skinn Robert	Harper Joshua	Harper Joshua		Wise Robert	Wise Robert
3.	Harper Edward	Harper Edward	Harper Edward		Harper Edward	Harper Edward
Dressmakers/ Sempstresses						
1.	Beilby Mary	Beilby Sophia	Booth Ann	Booth Ann	Girdley Emily	Girdley Emily
2.		Crowther Ann	Crowther Alice		Brooks Emma	Brooks Emma
3.		Wilkinson Jane	Newcombe Catherine			Wise Lucy
4.		Wray Hannah	Atkinson Eliza			Sainter Emma
5.			Sellars Emma			Marshall Mary
6.			Beilby Mary			Coverdale Gertrude
						Hill Alice
Millers						
1.	Beilby George	Beilby George	Beilby Henry	Marshall Thomas	Clayton John C.	Clayton John
2.		Beilby Rowland	Marshall Thomas	Small Robert	Clayton John W.	Clayton Foster
3.		Beilby Henry			Clay Daniel	Clayton Tom
4.					Clayton Foster	
5.					West William F.	
Carriers						
1.	Hodsman R. 1823	Featherstone James	Thompson Joseph		Bayram Joseph 1879	Dowson Wm. 1892
2.	Featherstone James 1840		Featherstone Wm. 1858		Hotham John 1882	
Shopkeepers						
1.	Clark Robert 1823	Andrew Elizabeth		Andrew Elizabeth 1872	Dyson Henry 1882	
2.	Kemp James 1823	Sellars Joel		Sellars Joel 1872	Thompson 1882	
3.	Andrew Elizabeth					

VILLAGE OCCUPATIONS IN THE NINETEENTH CENTURY

	1841	1851	1861	1871	1881	1891
Grocers						
1.	Westerdale George		Thompson Joseph		Anderson Selina 1882 [Also Beer Retailer]	Anderson Selina [Also Beer Retailer]
2.			Andrew Elizabeth			
Butchers						
1.		Ranson John	Bate Thomas	Westerdale George 1872	Westerdale George 1882	Atkinson G 1892
2.		Crowther Edwin	Sanderson Thomas			
Confectioners						
1.						Fryett Elizabeth 1889
Publicans						
1. The Malt Shovel	Quest John	Andrew Wm. Ag. Lab.	Featherstone John	Andrew Wm. Ag. Lab.	Watson Thomas Ag. Lab	Watson Wm. 1892
2. The Fleece/ White Horse	Drew Gabriel	Drew Gabriel 1855				
3.	Sellers Joel	Featherstone J. 1858		Arnott William 1872 / Harrison Wm. 1872	Newby Robert 1879	
Beer House						
1.	Featherstone James	Featherstone James				
Professional and Industrial						
1. Landowner / Barrister	Todd John	Todd John	Todd John	Todd John	Todd John	Todd John
2. Dental Surgeon			Kirby Richard			
3. Minister of Religion	Lewis John	Lewis John	Wishart James		Whitehead John	Whitehead John
4. Schoolteachers	Witty Richard / Witty Emma	Witty Richard / Thornton Elizabeth	Witty Richard / Witty Anna	Witty Richard	Witty Richard	Beynon William / Witty Richard Retd.
5. Industrialists	Thompson Henry Retd.		Duncan Andrew	Duncan Andrew	Duncan Andrew	Duncan Andrew Retd. / Sir James Reckitt

APPENDIX 5

Deaths in Swanland 1808 – 1815   Recorded by Samual Galland

Year	Month/Day	Name	Age on Death	Comments
1808	Oct. 26	John Turner		
	Nov. 16	George Brocklebank		
1809	Oct. 31	William Watson	41	
	Nov. 12	Raspen Ringrose	27	
	Dec. 9	Thos. Cratchard	59	
1810	Jan. 22	John Briggs	76	
	Nov. 20	Mrs Nell	55	
1811	Mar. 28			Mr Barkworths ship landed at Hessle Cliff
1812	Apl. 25	William Petfield	46	
	Apl. 28	John Crathom	44	
	May. 12	Thomas Lacey	56	
	May. 28	Robert Turner Madden		Drounded in Sistron
	May. 30	Thomas Dunn Sun		Drounded in Humber
	Jun. 13	Mrs Boater	76	
	Aug. 9	R. C. Broadley	74	
1813	Feb. 5	John Sykes	52	
	Jun. 22	Alice Clark	33	
	Sept. 16			John Featherstone child kiled. Sam Shaws wagon
	Nov. 8	Robert Toumner	34	
1814	Jan. 8	Robt. Todd	21	
	Jan. 16			Thos. Atkinsons daughter died. Burnt
	Feb. 25	Thomas Wittey		
1815	Feb. 6	Henery Boldran	59	
	Feb. 16	Rev Thomas Broadlay		
	Mar. 13	Mrs Newlove	66	
	Mar. 22	Mrs Hall	88	
	Oct. 16	Peter Hodsman	54	
	Dec. 21	Mrs Stephenson	65	At Ferriby Mill

INDEX

Fig 34   Reproduced from

The Ordnance Survey Map of Swanland 1888